Sebastian Coe, from his early triumph in winning the English Schools' 3000 metres championship at the age of sixteen, to world records in the 800 metres, 1000 metres and the mile, and gold and silver medals at the Moscow Olympic Games, has become the foremost middle-distance runner of our time. Despite an illness which threatened to mar his running career, he fought back again to win gold and silver in the 1984 Los Angeles Olympics.

Peter Coe recognised his elder son's extraordinary potential early on and has since dedicated himself wholeheartedly to his development and training. He is now a recognised authority on middle-distance running and lectures internationally on all aspects of coaching and training runners.

Running for Fitness

SEBASTIAN and PETER COE

SPHERE BOOKS LIMITED
London and Sydney

First published in Great Britain by Pavilion Books Ltd
in association with Michael Joseph Ltd 1983
Copyright © 1983 PNC
Published by Sphere Books Ltd 1984
30–32 Gray's Inn Road, London WC1X 8JL
Reprinted 1984

Editorial Consultant: Nick Mason

Set in Plantin

Printed and bound in Great Britain by
Collins, Glasgow

Contents

A Life of Running

When running has enriched the lives of two people as much as it has ours, and when it has done this in so many ways, the wish to share the pleasure is a very strong one.

We are well aware that while the super-enthusiast is happy in his own world, he is in danger of becoming a bore when he tries to convert others to his own beliefs. Why then should we presume to add to all the other books on running and fitness?

We enjoy the involvement in running at the very highest level. It is not a privilege that can be bought or conferred, it has to be won. It can be achieved only by starting at the bottom and then, with dedication, and resolution and hard work, climbing slowly to the top. As so often in life, the effort is at least as rewarding as the prize – for who can put a value on what has been learned on the journey?

The coach and the athlete not only become aware of the problems that face beginners, they also learn that superstars are not immune to the same problems, in some degree or other. And in facing difficulties that cannot be avoided on the way up they learn how to overcome them. This book is based upon what we have learned on that climb.

Running is a natural thing to do, and as every child runs, or wants to run, it might seem that there is not all that much to it, and not a lot that can be said about it. The first assumption is true, the second is not. There is a lot that can be said and written about running, and the problem is not what to put in but what to leave out.

Of necessity much of this book must contain plain facts and figures. Muscles have Latin names, different shoes have specific functions. But we are writing about more than this; we are writing about running: the whole is so much greater than the sum of its parts. Anyone who runs, at whatever level, will find that he is at the same time finding out about himself and, even through his running, making a personal statement. For many of the men and women now caught up in marathon running, this is especially true.

Running is running. Yet to many it is more than that, it is a way of life. In some parts of Britain for example, cross-country running is King. Its disciples would be adamant – world records and gold medals notwithstanding – that no runner has arrived until he has won the 'National'. You smile? Until you have seen a truly hard-fought National (and every one is hard-fought) with its giant field and its cavalry charge start, you cannot begin to appreciate the enormous pull of the National Cross-Country Championship to competitor and spectator alike. In the not too distant past, for many good track men, miling was something to do to fill in the summer until the real running began once more, and the road running scene which overlaps the seasons and has its own intense excitement, especially with the great distance relays, claims its own fanatical adherents.

The spectrum of the sport is astonishingly wide; from jogging at one end to attempting world records at the other. Between them there are such variations as orienteering, with its combination of navigation and stamina, which offers a unique challenge to those who would like to 'rally' without charging deep into our countryside in cars; or that most formidable challenge to nature at its most raw, the hard companionship of fell-running. Or, if all that sounds too competitive, remember that every kind of running, with perhaps the exception of track athletics, can be enjoyed at your level and in your way without competing against anyone but yourself. You can set out at any time you choose to run the country lanes or highways – you may set off down a hill or along a mountain ridge at your own pace. You are not compelled to race anybody. You can run solo with only a map, or a list of clues by which to navigate. At the end of the day the occasional well earned 'half' will be doubly welcome, but as you rise to your own challenge and reflect, justifiably, on your own modest attainments, achieved alone or in the company of other like-minded souls, you will know that these efforts have their own rewards.

For some, as we have said, running is a way of life. For others, regrettably, it can become more than that. It assumes the proportions of a religion or, worse still, becomes an addiction and an obsession, as its victims become unbalanced and hooked on mileage mania. From there running can all too easily become a substitute for living and a retreat from the real world – a sad aberration that is being reported with increasing frequency from the United States. Far from achieving the fitness and the sense of well-being that it should bring, it is more likely to end in a frustrating crop of over-use injuries and a lowered level of health from the constant over-stress.

Fitness must be sought after with care. In all the enthusiasm and perseverance we should not forget that in running the real achilles heel is excess. We must always keep the main objective in mind: to run for fitness, but to run for pleasure as well. It is ridiculous to confuse the need to maintain a running programme and its concomitant dedication with an obsessive drive to complete a schedule regardless of the consequences. The total commitment of an Olympic athlete to run in the once-in-a-lifetime final and to hell with the possible consequences is understandable – if not wholly wise – but for anyone else it is quite inexcusable. It was that great hurdler David Hemery who rightly said that a serious test of an athlete's quality is how he behaves when he is injured.

To urge competitiveness and to urge caution in quick succession is not a contradiction. The longer you keep running well the longer you will stay well. And if you are running for fitness, anything that curtails your running will also curtail your fitness. The basis for overall physical fitness is achieved by improving your respiration and your circulation, and to this end the most effective activity is running. Once this base is obtained it has to be maintained, and again it is running, though not necessarily in larger doses, that will do it effectively. Furthermore,

running's one great advantage is that it is not an expensive pursuit, and your sessions can be timed to suit yourself. In the unhappy event of your being unable to run for any length of time, the alternative methods of maintaining fitness – cycling, perhaps, or swimming, gymnasium training or even physiotherapy – tend to be less effective, more time-consuming and usually more expensive. In every way it is better to stay unhurt and fit.

This caution is as important in a coach as it is in a runner. Assisting and guiding an athlete to the pinnacle of his or her running success requires a hard and demanding taskmaster. But lasting success has never been achieved without understanding the need for moderation. In preparing training schedules for the build-up, the pre-race and the race periods, the correct restraint is at the very heart of the matter. When applying increasing doses of stress – for that is what a large part of race training is – giving the correct opportunities for recovery requires careful thought. And if the top performers can practise restraint in their training build-up, then so can fitness runners, for certainly the same pressures are not on them.

As runner and coach we have been involved in serious competitive running for fourteen years. Before that, as boy and father, we shared the child's joy of uninhibited running. Since we started serious competition we have also shared the ever-increasing discipline and pressure that continued success imposes. We have shared, too, in a different way, the pride of world records and the ecstasy and agony of victory and defeat in the Olympic Games. But in the end the true experience, and the self-knowledge that goes with it, belongs to the runner and to him or her alone.

This book is written in the hope that it will give encouragement and guidance to those who want to share in the unique experience that running can give. If it were to start some unknown on a personal quest to 'Go for Gold' it would be a delightful bonus. But it will bring equal satisfaction if someone starting out later in life, seeking no more than enjoyment, health and well-being, finds here the same encouragement.

AUTHOR'S NOTE
The greater part of the book represents the joint thoughts and opinions of both of us. In a few places where we have felt it more useful to include expert opinion or personal reminiscence particular to one or other of us, the change is clearly flagged and the first-person section set in different typeface.

Sebastian Coe
Peter Coe
Sheffield, England
Spring 1983

Why Run?

There have been very few, if any, societies in history which have not shown competitiveness in some way. It is hardly within the scope of this book to analyse social behaviour, but it is sufficient to say that sports and games have been with man for a very long time, and that in one form or another, running or jumping have always had their place.

For the majority of people in Western society the physical demands are minimal, and for many the mental demands are also decreasing. Today there are more and more people with more and more leisure – some of it earned, some of it enforced – who are bound to be faced with the problem of time on their hands. There is no real virtue in hard, gruelling work for its own sake, and one of the proper uses of technology has been to liberate mankind from drudgery. But in the Western world modern technology also offers the ordinary man a better diet than he has ever known, notwithstanding many of the junk foods that are on the market.

Thus we face the contradiction that we have enhanced nutrition that is not matched by an enhanced work load. Worse still, the modern man and woman have the additional problems of coping with the foodstuffs industry, from which a large amount of advertising is aimed at persuading people to eat for pleasure – a very different proposition from taking a normal, healthy pleasure in what they eat.

Modern society also tends to regard all problems as having technological solutions. Every doctor knows that many of his patients no longer regard sound advice as therapy, and without recourse to drugs or even surgery they do not believe they are getting good treatment. There are innumerable jars, bottles, tubes, capsules and syringes containing alleged cures and reliefs for ills that arise solely from the way we live. Consider how much orthopaedic trouble has arisen from fashion shoes alone. Think how many people insist on medicine and treatment rather than stop smoking. We owe it to ourselves, as well as to society, to try to live in a more natural and healthy way. There may not be much we can do about our employment, but there is a lot we can do with our diet and our leisure.

A carefully worked out running schedule, coupled with a good diet, will not only help us to achieve fitness, but it will also be one of the best pieces of preventive medicine that we ever undertake. That exercise is 'good for you' has long been believed, but the duration of a belief is not a proof. It has only been with careful long-term studies that solid evidence has become available.

There may indeed be a built-in human need for exercise. Living as we do in a Western industrial society, we tend to forget that there are still parts of the world where people live by hunting and foraging and even follow a nomadic existence, and that our own days as hunters and foragers are only in the very recent past. Before the intervention of modern science and technology, survival went only to the fit.

Both hunting and early agriculture involved hard work, which is exercise after all, and since survival then depended on strength, skill and mobility, it might very well follow that we are genetically programmed for physical work or exercise.

If the play of young animals such as puppies, kittens and cubs can be seen as part of their development, then the games children play might also be showing us the way we were intended to be.

We ensure that our pets are adequately exercised without drawing the proper conclusions from it. Animals confined in conditions that do not allow them adequate exercise become unhealthy and mean-tempered; it's a simple step to draw a parallel to humans. We strongly believe that the best base for mental health is physical fitness. It is worth reminding ourselves just what is the body's most important function. It is to feed and protect the brain, which houses the mind. Without the brain functioning properly we will lack not only an understanding of what we are doing, but also the necessary willpower to meet the demands of successful training. Furthermore, once fitness is achieved, it will need maintaining. *Mens sana in corpore sano* – 'a healthy mind in a healthy body' – is a much quoted proposition, as old as it is corny. But is no lesser an ideal for that, and it remains a neat and realistic conception of health: mental fitness linked to bodily fitness.

When finally listing reasons for running, which range from a biological need to avoiding the excesses of living, it is easy to appear puritanical without meaning to be so. This would be a great pity, because one of the attributes of running is the sheer pleasure of it. Running when undertaken sensibly is a fun thing. Even when some of the fun is driven out by the sheer intensity of the sessions that the most dedicated performers must undergo, the pleasure flows back with the feeling of achievement and the company of others in search of the same goals.

There are any number of valid reasons for wanting to run. Most of these will be totally personal, and could include emulation, mental escape, physical freedom, perhaps even friendship. But whether or not fitness is among your reasons, fitness you will certainly achieve.

As man is a gregarious animal it might well be that an athletic club could offer both the companionship and the advice and support that you feel you need when starting to run – and could be true even if you want to run for fitness rather than to compete. No jogger should feel that he is out of place in a running club: in our own club, the Hallamshire Harriers, there is a place for everybody, including the parents of young members. Indeed, there have been many cases of parents following in their children's footsteps and subsequently becoming active runners themselves.

Athletic clubs vary in size and quality, and the choice is yours. Being comprised of people, they are bound to have the odd crank among the membership, but they are just as likely to have a member or two who have made a study of some aspects of fitness, and who would be glad to help you. Our own club newsletter, which we happened to refer to when we were preparing this book, is compiled by an active veteran runner who finds time to compete, officiate and edit.

For coach and athlete at the highest level running is – and must remain – a very serious matter, and we cannot afford to be flippant when giving advice to others. But that doesn't mean that we have forgotten how much fun running can provide. For every race that fades from the memory into mere statistics, there is another of which the mere mention can start us laughing – if only in the safety of hindsight. Like the appalling mid-winter mudbath of a cross-country race in Derbyshire which started and finished in a bleak wooden hut as a changing room, to which the runners returned, half-frozen, to clean up under one common cold-water tap and with one enamel bowl. Or the potential misery of another bleak evening in the Dales when one of the cars broke down on the return journey to Sheffield. It was the wild, impromptu football match that whiled away the time until the car was repaired which remains in the memory, a match that served up more professional fouls in a deserted Derbyshire school-playground than can have been seen in the whole World Cup!

It wasn't all disaster, either. We shall never forget the international road race at Loughrea in Ireland, when the race was preceded by entertainment and dancing, and followed by a riotous evening in Galway of eating, dancing and incomparable Irish hospitality. Nor the complete contrast to that single cold Derbyshire tap – the day of the Batley road relays when the local swimming pool, complete with warm water, was thrown open to all the runners.

All over the country, every weekend, there are teams on the move taking their own fun and laughter to the competition. For us, bound tightly by our employment and by the work and detailed preparation required for top level international competition, there is far less time nowadays for such fun-and-games outings. But the wit and the laughter of those coach journeys has stayed with us longer than the events they accompanied, and if the glory still goes to the superstars, the most fun in running remains with the majority.

We all know the old saying – everything you enjoy is either illegal, immoral or fattening. Well, running certainly isn't any of these.

One Man's Return . . .

This is the tale of a friend of ours who proved to himself the hard way that being overweight and unfit can subject tendons and muscles to sudden loads that might be reasonable for the fit, but not for the sedentary. The belated preventive therapy that his case illustrates could hold good for anyone looking for a reason to run.

John Edwards is his name. He was our next door neighbour, and he had seen Sebastian as a thirteen-year-old set off on his daily training runs either on the road or round an all-weather football pitch. One day he said rather wistfully, 'I used to do a bit of running myself.'

John's profession was and still is demanding, but only mentally so. Lecturing in a university on control engineering taxes the head, not the body. In addition, and he will not mind us saying it, John has a gourmet's taste with a gourmand's delight for food. In short, he was well overweight. It was the classic situation when 'somewhere, somehow, something's gotta give'. It did – it was his knee.

It was a game of squash that was the turning point; in the middle of a rally he badly tore the tendons in his knee – a simple overload.

His stay in hospital gave him time to reflect upon his younger days and his sport when in the fourth, fifth and sixth years at school he ran cross-country. At university, too, he had run at least twice a week for three years, and while he never made the top, neither did he reach the thirteen stones that helped to finish his knee.

Emerging from his enforced rest lighter and wiser, John's interest in running was further heightened by seeing Eric Miller's fine film of the famous Three Peaks fell race.

He saw clearly that here was a chance to combine his love of nature and the outdoors with the need for enhanced fitness in a positive way. For him it became running for fitness and fell running for the challenge, with road-racing as a back-up sport.

His training is largely done solo. He enjoys running with groups as often as he can, and he would prefer to be with other runners, but the solo running, though harder, provides the solitude that gives him time to think over problems or ideas free from other distractions.

The roads and moors of Derbyshire and Yorkshire over which he trains, while magnificent, make very hard and demanding courses. Although used somewhat differently, it is the same area that stimulates Sebastian so much and provides the hard background mileage on which his training is based.

John commenced slowly, and he steadily built up his strength and stamina through a period of jogging before starting continuous running as part of his training. He now uses road-running and six-mile road races for sharpening his speed but when we asked him why, despite his respect for road speed, he loved fell running we got an interesting reply: 'I feel the macho image and the toughness of the challenge to be the extra ingredients that compensate for the lack of sheer speed.'

Even when involved with extra work, either setting or marking examination papers or other additional university demands, he maintains his training. Depending upon the terrain over which he is running, or on the state of his preparation for a race, his mileage can vary between thirty and fifty miles per week; over the year he maintains his forty-mile-a-week average. From being a regular tail-ender in racing and training, he is now moving up through the field. As he gets older his times keep improving, and he has not suffered any set-back from injury.

. . . and One Woman's Arrival

Family reaction to all this has been encouragingly positive. John's wife Margaret's earlier mild humour at John's truly desperate perseverence in the early days slowly gave way to an understanding and admiration, not just for him but for everyone who runs.

Her interest in running, like John's, had first been aroused by seeing the *Three Peaks* film and following the fortunes of their young neighbour, Sebastian. But initially she only dabbled (and this phase lasted for about three years), partly because she suffers from both migraine and asthma, and partly because of her family responsibilities.

Nevertheless, the day came when Margaret decided that brief insights into the advantages of feeling fit warranted going the whole hog and getting thoroughly fit, and running was to be the principal means of reaching this goal.

This time she was to adopt a more thorough approach. On her earlier outings she had found that running on the flat was one thing and that running up hills was quite another. In other words she was proving that if you have a weakness, hill running will find it. Hill running requires a good all-round fitness but also, like sprinting, it requires strength.

Now, because of the previously mentioned difficulties, Margaret looked for a fitness course that she could carry out at times most convenient to herself, and she chose the *Sunday Times Body Maintenance* fitness programme. Ignoring . both the sarcasm of her offspring and the advice of the *Sunday Times* to complete the women's programme first, she plunged straight into the men's course and soon adopted a minor running programme on top of it. Very pleased with the result of the *Sunday Times* exercises and, as she puts it herself, 'with all the bits that wobbled under control', she then took to a more serious running programme and to her great joy the hills that had once been insuperable were now quite manageable.

She now runs twice a week at least, and usually manages three outings a week – on Wednesday, Saturday and Sunday. If her work as a teacher allows, she also tries for a run at lunchtimes on Mondays and Tuesdays. A long run is between eight and ten miles, an easy run is four miles. The weekend runs are the ones she can use for distance and any three short runs will total at least fifteen miles.

It is the flexible kind of programme that a working wife and mother must develop.

What does she say now about her new-found fitness? 'Above all, I really do enjoy the extra sense of well-being that I have achieved. And because I was determined to do something about my general condition before I reached a

Margaret and John Edwards: from perseverance to pleasure

point of no return, the lifting effect on my wounded vanity was reward enough. The good effect on my appearance of the combined fitness exercises and the running is not so much in the reduced inches as in the increased muscle tone and the general firming up that goes with it.

'I have lost only a few pounds, but my shape is so much better. I recall the thrill of this first realisation. I was sitting watching the television. I stirred in my chair and felt firm new thigh muscles for the first time – Oh, the joy!

'Mentally I am better too. I have a lot more confidence in myself, and going for a run seems to get me over that "life has got me down" feeling, even if the run has to be at a time when I really don't want to go. I never regret going for a run, no matter how reluctantly I start out.'

She still has obstacles to overcome. She is still a migraine sufferer, and a headache induced by over-exertion can last all day; and her asthma, though controlled by drugs, is still there. But the children, who thought the running all a bit of a joke, don't laugh any more, and the comments from members of the public have lessened over the last two years, an indication in itself of the social acceptance of running for fitness – 'Anyway, I don't care any more.'

She was pleasantly surprised by the helpfulness of the seasoned and experienced runners who, provided they saw someone really trying, were very supportive, and keen to give help and good tips on running or injuries.

She enjoys running with John because it stretches her, although she is aware that he still has to slow down a bit for her. She is proud that she can run up some of the most testing hills, she has run as much as 15 miles, and she is now contemplating entering a half-marathon. Perhaps the fascination both John and Margaret Edwards feel for fell running can be explained by the size of the challenge.

The 'Big One' is in the Lake District where the standard is 42 peaks in 24 hours. The record is held by Bob Graham who has logged all 42 in 13 hours. Imagine three very hilly marathons including the equivalent of a trip up and down Everest.

In summary it is fair to say that running has changed a thirteen-stone injury-prone man into a very fit eleven-stone injury-free man with a racing weight a few pounds less. For Margaret, the rewards have been less dramatic, but equally satisfying. Could this be you?

These stories of men and women finding rejuvenation through running are not fairy tales made up by the shoe manufacturers. You may not want to fell-run – there's no reason why you should, but there are plenty of opportunities for people with every kind of outlook. Perhaps a good collective noun for fun and fitness beginners might be 'a Bassetts of Runners' – a collection of all-sorts. There will be all manner of shapes and sizes, and all of those who continue with the sport will refine their shapes and achieve a worthy goal.

The Women's Angle

It is easy to forget that the similarities of the sexes are much greater than the differences and in the same way that one can get an odd feeling seeing women's pages in newspapers, and journals labelled magazines for women – as if they inhabited a different world – it seems an odd idea to write a section on women.

As far as running is concerned, women are no different from men. They have become part of the running boom at all distances from fun runs to marathons and the fitness that running brings men, it will bring equally well to women. No longer is it difficult for a woman to find running shoes her size, no longer is the sight of a woman training through the streets an occasion for amazement and wolf whistles.

In competition, too, women have rightly begun to play a more important part. In the last fifteen years we have seen a significant increase in the range of official championship distances in women's events. On the track women run all distances up to 3000 metres, and there is soon to be an official 10,000 metre distance for them. On the road they run anything up to a marathon – and some even compete at the 'ultra' distances beyond that.

There are differences, of course. For young women runners pregnancy, and any effect that running might have on the pregnancy and vice versa, is bound to be an important consideration. As one would expect, through the political involvement of the state in sport, there has been more attention paid in the Eastern bloc countries than there has here to the success of women in sport, and also to their reintegration into competition after childbirth. The immensely detailed book *Track and Field*, published in East Germany in 1977 under the auspices of the Leipzig College of Physical Culture, has gone thoroughiy into the subject. In summary, their conclusions are that:

Intensive training before pregnancy does not cause difficulty with the first delivery, and the physical condition of the mother after childbirth is better and more stable than before the pregnancy. More than half the pregnant athletes they studied did not suffer loss of form in the first three months of pregnancy and they were allowed to train and compete under medical control.

Pregnant athletes suffering from nausea, sickness, hypertension or anaemia are not allowed to train or compete, but are advised to continue lighter exercise, like gymnastics and swimming.

For the second three months very light training – but not jumps or force exercises with sudden position changes – is encouraged. The light training is designed to keep up the general condition of the cardiovascular system. In the final three months, deep breathing, swimming and extended walks are recommended.

After delivery an immediate commencement of exercise for strengthening the abdominal and pelvic muscles is started and after one month strengthening exercises for the particular event, together with moderate endurance exercises. After three months the athlete can resume real exertion. It is considered that around six months after delivery she should be fit and trained well enough for competition.

The East German study also concludes that training on this pattern does not hinder breast feeding.

There are plenty of reports from America of women who have kept on running or jogging very late into pregnancy, but it should be remembered that the demands on these women will be a lot less than on those in competition, and in any case a woman in late pregnancy should be under medical supervision.

As we write there is further confirmation, this time from Great Britain. In 1978 Jane Colebrook (now Jane Finch) won the European indoor 800 metres championship in Spain. In January 1983, only eight months after her confinement, she convincingly won the WAAA indoor 1500 metre championship at Cosford. This was of particular interest to us, because at the 1983 Congress of the European Athletics Coaches' Association we heard the Russians report that their experience with women showed after the first child their whole organism stabilised and they were capable of enhanced performance, though there was no evidence that subsequent pregnancies continued to further improve athletic ability. All this should help dispel any lingering Victorian ideas that pregnancy is an illness rather than a healthy experience.

The so-called frailty of women is not the only myth to have built up around the comparatively recent entry of women into competitive athletics. Another, quite contradictory absurdity, has recently been gaining ground which, if taken seriously, might be harmful to sport in general and running in particular.

In the past, for various socio-economic reasons, women have failed to achieve their full athletic potential. Now that barriers are at last disappearing the overall performances of women – as one would expect – are improving rapidly, particularly in middle- and long-distance running. These achievements have led to statement like: 'by the year 2000 (or whatever crystal ball date you care to insert) women's records will equal the men's.' Quite simply this is not true.

In *The Physiology of Exercise*, Morehouse and Miller list forty-seven significant differences between men and women and to pick out only some of them is enough to prove the point. Men are stronger than women and, more significantly, their power-to-weight ratio is higher than women's. Their larger lungs and hearts, too, give enhanced vital capacities. Higher aerobic, anaerobic and oxygen-carrying capacities give physical advantages to males that are too big to be ignored.

When the surge due to social changes has finished, and the rate of improvement has levelled off, the very real physiological advantage of males will still be there and then we could be left with the following ridiculous proposition: Ms X achieves a magnificent all-time best performance. However, since she failed to get within so many seconds or minutes of Mr Y's world record, it is hailed not as a great performance, but as a worthy 'failure'.

It is not as silly as it may sound. In one of the finest track races of 1982 David Moorcroft beat Sidney Maree, John Walker, Steve Scott and the rest of a world-class field in a 3000 metre invitation at Crystal Palace, broke the European record for the distance and came within a second of the world best time. At least one national newspaper greeted the superb performance the next day with the headline 'Moorcroft's near miss'. And Sebastian too has won an international race in Europe, only to find his victory announced in England as a 'failure to beat the world record' – a record that he had set himself!

If the 'parity of records' nonsense was allowed to prevail it would prevent many women from going on to reach their full potential: nothing is more disheartening than struggling to achieve impossible and unrealistic targets. Women's times will approach more closely to men's but they will not exceed them. In long-distance events women stars are able to beat many men runners, because the spread of ability in any population group is very wide. But these performances are general, and world records are very specific.

For some time, for reasons both chauvinistic and political, it has been easy to excuse the relative failure of Western athletes compared with those of the Eastern bloc in the race for medals and world records. The reasons given have ranged from drug abuse to state-supported professionalism. State aid, it is true, can be a great help, particularly when there is a state back-up in sports medicine, but it most certainly is not the whole story. Now, with the emergence of brilliant all-round athletes like Daley Thompson, and the grip taken on all the middle-distance records by Coe, Ovett and Moorcroft, all from a small country like England, these excuses are beginning to look decidedly weak, especially as the emergence of younger men like Steve Cram is providing world-class continuity.

So we are now left with another set of female myths. One says: 'You can't succeed at the top and still look like a woman.' (It usually comes clothed in remarks like 'Oh, well – if you want to look like a man.') Another is: 'Do you want to be as big as that?' Or 'They're not really women, are they?' – comments both stupid and wounding.

There will always be people who take steroids illegally, willingly or under some coercion, but this does not account for all the Eastern European success in the women's events – the publicity will always go to the grotesque rather than the normal. But there are world-class female athletes from all countries whose only 'abnormality' is super-fitness and extremely healthy looks. They are attractive and clear-skinned, they do not carry around unwanted fat, and they do not look like men. Exercise, particularly running, does not detract in any way from physical attraction in women, it can only enhance it.

It is not without interest that the very countries which are under attack for doping their way to success (for which there are proven examples and no excuses) also provide excellent advice for women athletes on menstruation and pregnancy, right through to how to resume an athletic career after childbirth, and with a record of improved performances to show for it.

It is one thing to have a firm and valid objection to a political system; it is quite another to shut your eyes and rationalise your failure. All that is required for the women in Britain to join the men of their country at the very top is to show the same will and commitment to succeed. The training knowledge is here, the success should be with it.

The Choice is Yours

For men and women alike, the time is likely to come when plodding around the local streets or the local park is going to lose its fascination, and you will be thinking of branching out into something more specialised. All the following forms of running – whether you are attracted by the competition they can provide or the companionship or the relaxation they offer – will give a whole new dimension to your search for fitness.

Road Running

Almost every section in this book will deal with some aspect of road running – indeed, even the most inexperienced keep-fit runner will have had some experience of, at least, running on pavements – but road-racing is a widely popular sport, and a few words are important for a newcomer.

The spread of distances in competition is enormous, from around three miles to the marathon. And beyond that there are the ultra-distance races and the long place-to-place runs like the London-to-Brighton. Other forms of running are either on closed courses or in open country fairly remote from roads, but road running is on the public highway. It is vital to learn the rules of the sport and to stick to them. In some areas the police are extremely co-operative, but there is already one chief constable who looks upon road runners with as little favour as football crowds.

It is not worth giving ammunition to the prejudiced. Not all motorists see the runner as a healthy competitor doing his own thing on the public highway. They are equally likely to regard you as a mobile obstruction carrying the sole responsibility of avoiding contact with their vehicle. Accidents tend to provoke the simple response from authorities. It is easier to stop people racing on roads than to restrain car drivers.

If you keep to the correct side of the road, do not cut corners or run straight across at intersections without looking about you, and adhere to any signs or instructions from the marshals, all will be well. But if you lose concentration you are the one who gets hurt. One more thing. If you are ever roped in for marshalling *stay alert*. A misdirection, or no directions at all, may not only send a runner off course and lose him a race – it could also send him out of the human race altogether.

Track Running
This is undoubtedly the showpiece of the sport, the branch of athletes from which the heroes and heroines of running are bound to emerge, from which the record books are written, and from which television draws so much of its sports audience.

A struggle for supremacy watched by millions on television

In all other forms of competitive running, comparisons between races are very difficult to make. No road course is the same as another and cross-country courses are even more dissimilar. You can only get a rough assessment of ability by comparing your position at the finish with those in a number of other races over the same distance. Track racing, though, offers far better opportunities to assess your own improvement.

Track running, too, has graded races. These are events which cater not just for the stars, but for those who have achieved a particular time for their event. For example, if your time for 800 metres is 2min 2sec your race will contain runners whose personal best time is close to this. Finishes are closer and more exciting, and these races provide the best experience in the early days of track competition. They give a better chance of winning, and no runner is going to be embarrassed by being beaten out of sight.

The humble runner who enjoys competition without having a great ability or the opportunities for a lot of training will also be able to run in club and open handicaps – another way of ensuring a more equal competition, and thus a greater chance of succeeding.

Track racing also has the advantage of an almost instantaneous feed-back by way of the observers. While the competitor can have a good feel for the condition of the runners close to him, the observer is in a much better position to read the race as it unfolds. The manner of a run, the degree of commitment, for example, or the changes of pace will often reveal as much about runners' strengths and weaknesses as the actual finishing time for the race.

It is one of the advantages of club life to have keen, supportive friends who want you to win and who can also give you a fair, unbiased account of your race. Even if you win it is important to know who was finishing quickly, and who may perhaps have been guilty of a tactical error earlier in the race, something worth knowing for the next time you meet. All this information helps you to assess the quality of your own performance, and only on the track is this possible.

In winter, for a privileged few, track racing moves indoors – a season which culminates this side of the Atlantic in the European Indoor Championships in March. The standard track is half the distance of the outdoor one – two hundred metres, slightly banked to allow for high speeds on the tighter bends. Many European and American cities have adequate indoor tracks, but only at Cosford, near Wolverhampton, courtesy of the RAF, can Britain boast an indoor circuit. It follows, inevitably, that for the average fitness runner, winter exercise is almost certain to be taken outdoors.

Cross-country Running

If you are the type who likes a good run for his money, then cross-country running will certainly meet your needs.

Look at the requirements: speed with endurance, strength with stamina, and the ability to change style and pace to suit the conditions. Quite a specification – but before you think of winning the National you will need a bit of experience.

A good tactical sense is essential in all kinds of running, and at 800 metres, as we well know, he who hesitates is lost. But even at 5000 metres, and 10,000 metres, when the leading bunch is on the attack, the complexities of pace-change are not as difficult to cope with as in a cross-country. For a start, conditions on the track are uniform from start to finish, and you can nearly always see the leaders; in cross-country the slopes and hills, the bushes and trees and sharp corners can soon obscure the leaders from the pack. In a road race there may be bends, but the field does not bunch up while it filters one at a time through a narrow gap as it often does in the country.

Up the steep slope, down the slippery bank, through the mud – the course is always changing. If any form of racing needs a good apprenticeship, this does. Experience of the traps and pitfalls and the many combinations of hazards that different courses provide is essential if you are going to do well.

Training for cross-country needs diligence and imagination to find opportunities to experience the sort of conditions you are likely to find in a race.

From the age of twelve, until the time he was eighteen, cross-country provided a grand toughening and testing background for Seb. It helped us to lay the foundation of his strength and stamina over a wide range of distances, and even today the sport provides its share of fitness and fun. And whatever the standard of the field, cross-country makes a grand day out for all, competitor and spectator alike. Regardless of the conditions, a fast, hard-fought race cannot fail to be exciting, and the refreshments after the race and the prize-giving that follows invariably provide warmth, wit and a lot of laughs.

A brief note to parents: give all the support you can to the school races, and the boys' and girls' events in the clubs. Support and encourage, but in your excitement do not push the youngsters too hard. Seb started at twelve, but it took him several attempts to get a good place in an English Schools' Championship at cross-country; if the youngsters are really keen, remind them that it is only as a senior that the wins really start to matter. A disheartened apprentice will never complete his indentures.

And a safety note for all competitors and the parents of young aspirants: make sure you are up to date with your tetanus immunisation. We have only one public track in Sheffield, the centre of which is often used for soccer matches and which frequently serves as the start and finish of our county cross-country championships. Despite the risks of tetanus, the corporation allows it to be used for equestrian events. Remember, don't blame a farmer if you fall or get spiked in or near manure.

Don't let the big mileages or the hard training necessary to shine in big cross-country races put you off. Even if you are only on thirty miles a week you will still be able to finish a four-mile or six-mile run. You won't be one of the first into the finishing funnel, for sure, but after a couple of tries it will be up to you if you want to push on. And however you perform there will always be an excited group of spectators at the finish, and their cheers never fail to lift the runners as they approach the line. Even the weariest of competitors can find the spirit for a final spurt at the end.

Fell Running

All devotees can wax lyrical over the attractions of their own sport, and in some sports the appeal is not always readily seen. But for those who want to add not only extra toughness and some degree of solitude to their sport, but also an extra touch of risk, join John Edwards and have a go at fell running.

Run nigh on full tilt down a loose scree hill, or down a mountainside with all certainty of safe footfall removed; add the vagaries of the weather, the very real possibilities of mist . . . and you will see that this sport demands a certain type of competitor.

No wonder John finds it has a macho appeal. If you are keen to join this hardy breed and flourish with them in their beloved wildernesses, you will find that the basic running gear, as well as the basic observations about training and safety, are the same as for cross-country, though special attention must be given to footwear.

Orienteering

No runner will get very far if he doesn't know where he is going. In cross-country or road running it is easy for competitors to run off-course if the route is not well marked, or if there are not 'markers' to call loud and clear directions to the competitors. Well organised races will have reduced this hazard to a minimum, so that even the front runners will be able to follow the course with ease, and can therefore concentrate on their running.

In orienteering, things are quite different. Finding the way is the name of the game, and navigation in woodland and forest is every bit as important as the running. The sport had its origins in military training in the forests of Scandinavia at the turn of the century, and has evolved as an increasingly popular sport in many parts of Europe, particularly in the last twenty-five years.

Orienteering is racing, but runners start at timed intervals, and create their own 'courses' by navigating from point to point by means of map and compass between a fixed start and finish. The points on the map they must visit are listed on a description sheet, and all are indicated on the map the runner carries with him. At each control – distinguished on the ground by a marker flag – he punches his card to prove he has found it, and proceeds to the next control and so on to the finish. It is not – take our word for it – as easy as it sounds.

Though the courses are not particularly long, the terrain can be demanding. It may be that the same degree of physical training is not required for orienteering as for competitive cross-country or road racing but the top exponents will probably be running fifty miles a week in training, and the sport undoubtedly demands more mental sharpness on the day; mental alertness declines as a runner gets tired, and a tired orienteer is many times more likely to lose his way – and with it valuable minutes on the clock – than a relaxed and strong orienteer. We would advise a full programme of distance, fartlek (see page 56) and interval training, and even speed-endurance running if you have any aspiration to top class results.

As with so many facets of running, much of the attraction of the sport comes from the fact that it is open to performers of all abilities. The Southern, the Midland and the Northern Championships, the British Championship itself, and the sport's great four-day Easter Festival, the Jan Kjellstrom Trophy meeting, are all open to all-comers, where the humblest beginner can compete in his or her age group against the best entrants from Britain and Europe – and get lost in the same part of the forest.

The best introduction to the sport is through local clubs, most of which organise Come-And-Try-It events from time to time. Almost any running gear will do to begin with, though it is a rule of the sport that all competitors are covered from neck to toe (primarily to avoid infections being passed on in overgrown, bramble-ridden areas where the same thorns might scratch different skins – it has happened! – but more practically to prevent the unnecessary shredding of skin in rough country). Tough, lightweight tops and trousers are designed for regular competitors, and there are a number of brands of shoe specifically designed for orienteering. Running over rough terrain with one eye on the map and the other searching for landmarks does not give you a lot of time to study your footfall – your feet are going to need the best grip, and the best support, that they can get.

Whether you start running solely for fitness or with the intention of racing, sooner or later this thought will enter your mind: 'How do I compare with others of my kind?' And why not?

There is a real joy at the end of a grand competitive effort, and the losers will have the full respect of the winner. It will not matter that on the way there you may have looked a little less than a golden Olympian, because you will share this truth with most of the others, and as anyone who has tried racing will tell you, the first time you pass another runner a never-to-be-broken spell is cast.

You can both be tired, puffing and wheezing, but the one who can drag himself a few extra inches per minute in front of the other walks tall until the next time.

'I developed a love of running as a child. I made my entry into the ranks of "serious runners" as early as the age of thirteen – half my life ago. I have been hooked, or perhaps snared, ever since. My entry into international athletics developed from that initial enjoyment I found from simply putting one foot in front of the other at anything faster than walking pace. Then, as now, the faster I ran the more exhilarating it became.

My immediate aim now is further success at the highest levels of the sport, but in my life as a runner, this will be only a temporary phase; I am sure the pleasure of running will not stop with my retirement.

I know that the same things that first attracted me to running – before the competitive side of the sport took over with all the glorious unpredictability that has gone with those select few years – will still be there, and I will once again be able to get back to the simple pleasure of going for a run. The enjoyment of the scenery will still be there, and so will the knowledge that I am keeping up – even at a somewhat lower level – the kind of all-round fitness that enhances everyday life.

It seems to have become fashionable in the last few years to package the joys of taking to the road in the manner of the wild-west salesman, extolling the virtues of their all-curing potions. America, particularly, has been subjected to a barrage of the all-curing claims of running: everything from constipation to cancer can be overcome by putting one foot in front of the other.

I am not making these claims, but it is true that at times of mental stress, whether academic or personal, taking to the trails has always been refreshing and helpful to me. I feel healthier and generally more resilient when in training, and the habit of the daily run will be with me for ever.

The rewards of a carefully planned and tempered fitness routine may not be felt immediately – indeed, you might even feel worse before you feel better. A level of fitness that will last will not be produced overnight, and the efforts that you make towards that goal are unlikely to progress without occasional periods of physical and mental strain.

But if you do feel discomfort please take heart. Every seasoned athlete at any level of sport will have gone into, and passed through, this phase. I always get this feeling when I make the transition between my winter work and the first few faster sessions on the track during springtime. But once I have climbed from this plateau of fitness on to the next, and I have equipped myself for the rigours of international competition, there is no denying the benefits. In just the same way, you will feel the satisfaction of knowing that you have left the land of the tired and breathless and have, by your own endeavours, joined the ranks of the fit.'

Starting Up

Once the helter-skelter running of childhood ceases, a general slowing up of the body begins. For some this process is delayed by organised sport and games in schools but, alas, for many, late adolescence sees the end of regular exercise. This has never been more true than today, with large sections of the population slumping into a television sloth at earlier and earlier ages. So now is the time to begin.

In the sense that it is always easier to maintain fitness than to achieve it, age *is* important for anyone thinking about running. It is a good example of the sooner the better, because if you do leave it too long, it could become too late. The best advice is to form good habits at a time when it is easiest to form them, but that said, there are several cases of men starting to run in their fifties and sixties and going on to run in marathons.

Age also offers a loose guide to the level at which you should start running, and the rate at which you should progress. We say 'loose' because any age group will be made up of individuals with widely different fitness levels. When you are thinking about fitness running you would be wise to start considering at the same time whether or not other aspects of your life are conducive to the fitness you are seeking. Running will take effort and time, and it does not make sense to waste either of them in a busy life. Attention to diet is important, and sleep is necessary – the more exercise you do, the more recovery you are going to need. However, slothful dozing in armchairs at every opportunity is neither wise nor necessary – it is probably best described as interval training for death.

Early days: Seb at 14, Sheffield Schools 1500-metre champion

'Do I need a health check?'

Before they start running some people will understandably be anxious about their health. Running may be good for my health, they will think, but is my health up to running? The answer to this is in two parts. First, those at risk from making a sensible and careful start to jogging and running are few (it is worth noting that, under medical advice, diabetic and epileptic runners for example, compete successfully at a high level). Secondly, running programmes have been used very successfully for the rehabilitation of patients, including those who have had heart trouble.

'Risk', for runners, is generally meant to be the degree of expectation of coronary illness. Most other ailments are so limiting that pain or decreased mobility would prevent running as an exercise until cured. Diseases of the lungs, for which you should certainly be receiving medical attention anyway, would preclude running for fitness until a doctor gave you the go-ahead.

Who would be in the categories at risk? Anyone who could not pass a stress electro-cardiogram test (known widely as a stress ECG). Other clinical tests would give strong contra-indications, including an ECG taken at rest, but a stress ECG would be the most conclusive. Unfortunately, the average person in Britain would neither know where to obtain, or want to bother himself with, this test. So apart from a routine check with your GP who, if he was sufficiently sports minded and had doubts about you, might recommend a stress ECG, the following list gives an indication of factors that you should consider if you are an inactive person or one not taking regular exercise:

Family history: do you have relatives who have had heart troubles?

Personality: are you a hyped-up go-getter? Is your working day a long one in a stressful environment?

Obesity: are you overweight? The condition places an unwelcome and unnecessary strain on the heart.

Smoking: the habit is often indulged in by those under real, or imaginary, stress. Heart attacks are more often fatal with smokers than with non-smokers, and among those who die from heart attacks the life span is dramatically shorter for those who are heavy smokers.

Blood Pressure: high blood pressure increases the risk of rupturing arteries.

Generally: anyone who feels at all distressed by increased efforts of a normal kind – stairs, gardening or hurrying for the bus – should seek medical advice before starting to run.

In short, prevention is always better than cure. If you have any doubts see a doctor first.

In a free world, we all have a choice in most things, and to whom you go for your medical advice is one such choice. It is important that you choose your physician carefully. Try to find one who will give you all-round advice, fairly presented. Our own orthopaedic specialist is candid in both diagnosis and prognosis, and he spells out the choices and what you may expect from them.

He freely acknowledges that his own love of winter sports will eventually result in a permanently fixed ankle. He thinks the cost is acceptable to him.

If you need medical advice, then seek it comprehensively, but while you need this knowledge, remember that it *is* advice, and that the decision must be yours. A good doctor will *want* to help you.

We shall have more to say later about the effects of smoking, but to anyone who argues for ignoring the warnings about smoking and health on the basis that there is no direct proof – only statistical evidence – we offer the following observation: insurance companies and betting organisations live by statistics, and very well too, it would seem. Why be a punter with your own life?

Getting Moving

It would be possible to break down the population into groups representing various categories of age, sex and initial fitness and to prepare running schedules for all these people, but that would require a book of its own. We propose to tackle three groups of men and women, all of whom we presume to be in normal health.

The first group is all those who are aged thirty and under, the second those between thirty and forty, and the last group all those over forty. Any divisions you care to make will be riddled with exceptions. Clearly a forty-four-year-old living outside London who leaves his or her cycle at the station each morning having ridden the four miles from home, and who plays the occasional game of squash after work, will be a lot fitter than a twenty-nine-year-old who does little or nothing beyond walking the dog to the pub.

However, the under-thirties should be able to start a modest jogging programme immediately, and the next group should be able to ease themselves into jogging with a little extra care and preparation.

The over-forties probably represent the group with the widest range of fitness, and therefore need the greatest care in starting up. Provided that there is nothing sufficiently wrong to exclude them from trying, the approach we recommend should enable anyone to get started on the road to fitness running. But for these men and women we do propose a very simple and careful beginning. If you are young enough or fit enough you can start more ambitiously, but remember, exercise was never spoiled by caution.

The Warm-up

Serious athletes will always warm up before an event, and part of their warm-up procedure will include stretching and suppling. Even brisk walking, if you are not accustomed to it, will cause the legs to tighten up a bit and some suppling exercise will help you to avoid, or at least alleviate, the effect of stiffening up after exercise.

There are reflex actions built into our nervous system which are designed to protect our joints and muscles from damage due to over-stretching. This reaction is triggered off to work before harm is done. However, if stretching is done jerkily, particularly with muscles cold or not well exercised, this protective reflex can itself be the cause of injury. So when muscles are being stretched so that the limbs can have an increased range of movement, it is much safer if this is done by static stretching – that is, slowly and comfortably getting to the limit of stretching, and then holding the position for ten to fifteen seconds. In this way you will not invoke the stretch reflex, and the increase in the range of movement will be safely achieved without muscle damage. If flexibility exercises are part of your warm-up routine, do not do them first. Gently jog around until you feel warmer, *then* do the exercises, after which you can continue your warm-up.

When you start exercising seriously, either for the first time or after a long lay-off, there are specific areas that will need extra attention.

For those approaching jogging via walking, it is advisable to include a number of exercises specifically for walkers – which partly overlap with those more suitable for middle- and long-distance runners. Walkers need to concentrate particularly on shoulders, spine, hips and ankles, whereas runners are more likely to be concerned with the hips, ankles and knees as the key areas. But since modern living hardly encourages us to use our bodies through their full range of movement, a full range of flexibility exercises is best for everyone.

First steps

There is an old proverb which says that it is better to learn how to walk before you try to run. This is good advice for older beginners, or for people who have dieted enough to feel ready to run.

First, let at least two hours elapse from your last meal. Blood is diverted to the stomach, away from the muscles, after eating; if you begin exercising too soon, the blood will be diverted away from the stomach to the muscles before it has finished its work, which can give rise to extreme discomfort in the stomach. Wear the shoes you are going to wear for running. Now you are ready to start.

Sedentary people have pulse rates of something between seventy and eighty beats a minute, and to sustain double this rate without discomfort is a good indicator of your condition and your progress. Begin by taking a fixed distance of one mile on a smooth, level path or pavement and walk this distance as briskly as you can without undue discomfort. Drawing deep breaths for a change is all right, panting and wheezing is not. As a guide a brisk pace would be four miles (6.5 kilometres) per hour, or one mile in fifteen minutes.

Immediately you reach the end of your walk check your pulse rate. Count for fifteen seconds and multiply by four, to give you the number of beats per minute. On successive walks, still maintaining an even pace throughout, increase the pace until you achieve a pulse rate of 140–150 per minute. From this point you can go on to extend the length of your walk to a mile and a half, and then two miles – always at an even pace. It is worth checking your pulse at one-mile, or even half-mile intervals, just to make sure you are maintaining this pulse rate throughout the walk.

It is worth making one further safety check. After you have finished your fast walk, allow five or six minutes for recovery, preferably still moving, but quite slowly. If as a beginner your pulse rate has not fallen to 120 beats per minute, then (if your finishing pulse rate was taken accurately) your effort was probably too hard.

Once you have found that you can walk for thirty minutes at a pulse rate of 140–150 per minute, you can extend this in easy stages until you can keep going steadily for one hour. You are now covering about four miles, and as you progress you will find that your pulse rate is falling, that is, you are covering the same distances in the same times with a decreasing pulse rate. You are now showing increased fitness and you are ready to try jogging. You will have certainly become used to your running shoes by now.

If at any time you suffer a chest pain, or giddiness or nausea – stop. You are either training too hard or these are symptoms of illness. If a chest pain should occur again on the next occasion you train, see a doctor as soon as possible. This is an obvious precaution, but you would have to be pretty far gone already to be injured by careful exercise.

'How much should I train, and how often should I train?' These are the questions that everybody asks sooner or later. Walking is not as stressful as running and it is a different action, so if you are starting by going through the walking phase, train every day if it is comfortable, or perhaps two days on and one off if you find you need some recovery time when you first begin.

Housewives, or people working short hours or part time, may find it possible to work out twice a day. A good walk or jog morning and evening is fine once you have become accustomed to exercise.

Provided that these simple checks on your condition are maintained as you progress, this should constitute a safe and simple introduction to aerobic exercise. As your programme increases so will your health, but always keep an honest eye on yourself – not the neurotic vigilance of the hypochondriac, but the sensible check on over-enthusiasm.

Now you are ready to jog. You have found that walking at an increased pace for an hour is no longer taxing (maybe you were one of the fitter ones anyway) and you want to push on. Right, get changed, warm up and go out. Start walking briskly and then increase the pace until you feel it would be easier to break into a slow run, which is what jogging is. Continue at this pace until the fatigue is moderately uncomfortable. At that point start walking again. Repeat alternate walking and jogging when you have recovered sufficiently.

There will then come a moment when you feel it becomes too uncomfortable to start jogging again. This time walk all the way back home. Next time you go out and on each successive outing, extend the jogs and the total distance.

This is the old boy scout way of alternate running and walking by which you increase your daily distance in your own way at your own rate of progress.

This jog-walk method offers you the broadest approach to continuous running with the choice of three immediate goals – duration, distance and continuous running. For example, if your goal is half-an-hour of continuous movement you walk-jog until this time is achieved after which you progressively shorten the walking periods until you achieve the full thirty minutes of continuous jogging, or you can set up a target distance, say three or four miles; then you shorten the walking recovery periods until you complete three or four miles of non-stop running.

We feel that the first aim – duration – will provide the best basis for distance running. This, after all, is what we are aiming at and in aerobic training, once a pulse rate around 140–150 is achieved, duration is the aim. Although our genetic inheritance is the ultimate decider of our running ability, endurance is somewhat easier to foster than speed, and in any case endurance is the better base on which to build.

Building Up Distance

For those who want to go on to compete, building up running distance must be the aim. Ultimately, what constitutes fitness will be decided by you, and for us to say you should reach this goal or that would be quite arbitrary. It would over-extend some and perhaps place a false limit on others. But for anyone who has the time and inclination to measure their progress carefully, and who likes testing themselves and securing points against a table, they could well use a graduated (and cautious) training programme, like the one suggested by Kenneth Cooper in his excellent book *The Aerobics Way*.

However, for that non-existent average man, middle-aged, middle-active and middle-weight, a weekly mileage of around twenty-five miles would be enough to help him keep a lot healthier than those who do not run.

Fitting in twenty-five miles of running into your weekly routine should be no great problem. If you take two days off running each week, you are left with five miles each, or five times thirty-five to forty-five minutes. Allowing for changing and freshening up, all you need is to set aside one hour a day at the most, five times a week.

Those who have adequate lockers and facilities at their place of work are the luckiest, because being able to run to or from work is a great advantage. It is healthier and cheaper at the same time. Alternatively if your commuting distance is too long, fitting in some lunchtime training may be possible. The weekends generally offer more opportunities for running, and a six-mile run on both Saturday and Sunday would leave only three more runs of four miles each during the week, say thirty minutes per run.

When broken down like this the total doesn't appear so formidable, and remember, all over the country there are runners logging up totals from forty to eighty miles per week and living normal lives.

A Place to Run

Where should I run? What surface should I run on? These are almost the same question. It is easy to list the desirable qualities of where to run, but in modern urban living it would be rare to find the perfect combination of the ideal and the practical.

Beginners should start running on smooth surfaces which are as true as you can find. This is the time when ankles and feet, which are unaccustomed to running and have not had time to strengthen, are at their most vulnerable. Until you have become used to running on uneven surfaces, try to keep to good paths or on grass that you can trust. Having to look carefully at every footfall while running is boring, and it could get you set into a bad style. By all means scan the ground ahead of you, but keep your head up – if your surroundings are pleasant, enjoy them. While good smooth grass is the best surface on which to run it does mean that you have to live near large open parkland. The paths in most urban parks are well maintained, and they offer the next best choice.

If as an inner city dweller you are forced to be a road runner there are some important do's and don'ts you should observe.

The first requirement is to stay away from main road traffic as much as possible. The concentration required to avoid being run over, particularly when going round parked cars, makes it difficult to slip into the kind of running detachment which makes for pleasure in running. A runner can get into a complete mental and physical rhythm – running on auto-pilot – that allows you to complete a run leaving your body healthily worked and your mind refreshed. This is neither easy nor safe on busy roads, and busy pavements are by definition impossible places for safe and satisfying running.

Wherever and whenever main road running is necessary, if at all possible avoid them at peak traffic hours. Running to and from your place of work is fine, but a heavy concentration of cars and lorries means a heavy concentration of exhaust gases; carbon monoxide is poisonous, and so is the lead in petrol fumes. Find the quietest roads you can, and if they are free enough the pavements are the best to run on. You may have to step off when you cross junctions but the pavement will be flatter than the road, which will have a camber.

If you are near to rural or semi-rural roads, then of course you will run in the road. The classic golden rule of running in the road is: face the oncoming traffic except when this would mean running on the inside of a tight bend, when you cannot be seen and cannot see what is coming.

Unfortunately what is good for road safety is bad for your legs. Continual running on a sloping surface is very likely to set up imbalance injuries – stress fractures are not unknown and knee pains are common, and there is a marked tendency to a sideways tilt of the pelvis and the lumbar region of the spine.

Running on the crown of the road reduces this risk, but substitutes that of being hit in the back by a lorry. The next best thing you can do is to alternate between sides, say every half mile, and look carefully when you switch over.

In summer, with longer hours of daylight, your choice of courses or routes is wider. Winter running restricts this choice to adequately lit roads. Determined runners, who believe they have good night vision and who wear bright reflecting clothing or over-vests, do go night running. Their precautions may even extend to a small bulb at their back, powered by a battery attached to a belt. Night running on unlit roads with its attendant risks is a personal decision, but what might drive a top competitor to train regardless is not so necessary to a fitness runner.

Crisp dry snow that is not too deep is good to run on. The higher knee lift required is strengthening and good for your running action, and the additional effort can be as hard as you want to make it. The general atmosphere is cheerful and refreshing, particularly when you are out with a group. But it does have a few hazards of its own. Don't run on unfamiliar ground. Don't run unless you have a good idea of what is under the snow. If there is only a thin layer of powdery snow on the grass or tarmac this is fine, but an apparently smooth layer of snow merely covering hard and rutted ice can be dangerous. You may not actually fall over or slide into an obstacle, but there are other ways of getting athletic injuries. In these conditions a runner instinctively tries to curl his toes into the ground to scratch for traction. This can give rise to shin splints, soreness in the fibula or a very 'bruised' feeling in the feet. All these injuries are common from running on uneven, hard-packed snow. Groin strain from trying to stop legs from slipping away sideways is another danger and in our experience these ill effects last a long time, sometimes as much as six to eight weeks. The more obvious risks are low park railings, sometimes only inches off the ground, or lightly covered pot-holes. If you are likely to be running in snow in winter, it is worth studying the ground in the autumn.

In extreme snow and ice, in order to run at all, you may have to wait until traffic has lessened and use a restricted course on roads that are well cleared and gritted.

This kind of restriction necessarily cuts down your choice of route. Varying your runs between flat and hilly courses not only adds variety but should be an essential part of the correct application of the running load. Top athletes know the advantages of phasing hard and easy sessions, and the beginner should not make every run the same length or tackle it with the same intensity.

The degree to which you need and seek variety in your routes depends entirely upon yourself. You must explore your own areas thoroughly and with imagination. When training in Sheffield finding hills is never a problem; in Loughborough this is quite another matter. You know your own area best.

If you decide to do your running on the local track, please respect it. Unless you are a sprinter and need to practise bend running or relay handovers in marked-out zones, or you need accurately measured distances for comparative times in sets of repetitions, there is very little need for training on tracks. But if you must use the track for winter lighting, freedom from traffic or whatever, please keep out of the two inner lanes. These are habitually churned up by people plodding round, getting in the way of those who are using the facility properly. On cinder tracks this is a nuisance; on synthetic tracks the cost of relaying the principal lanes, particularly the inside lane, is considerable. If you feel you must know exactly how long one lap is when running in any of the outer lanes, just measure the distance from the inside edge of the track to the centre of the lane you have chosen, subtract 30cm (one foot) and multiply by 6.286. Add 400 metres and this is the length of your lap.

The change of scene so important in avoiding boredom is rather easier at weekends, and more so in the summer. If you have a car, drive out into the country, and use an ordnance survey map to look for suitable rights of way or large estates open to the public – which could provide pleasant running surroundings. Indeed, for any runner looking for fresh routes the ordnance survey maps are worth an hour's study; and booklets describing country walks often include stretches that would make suitable running routes – sometimes fields, sometimes roads, sometimes both.

Such spaces as Chatsworth in Derbyshire, Clumber Park in Nottingham-shire, Wimbledon Common and Richmond Park in Surrey, and the Downs in

Sussex are all attractive and explorable. Coupled with a picnic such places could provide a pleasant compromise between a family weekend outing and an agreeable new running experience.

It might also give a husband and wife the chance to run together – something that varying work patterns often make difficult at other times. But even during a busy week it might make a pleasant change to run together – and might solve the potential problems for women running unescorted on the darker winter evenings.

Stretching Exercises

We all of us, athlete and non-athlete, share with the animals a common experience of stretching, particularly after sleep – it is the natural way of easing ourselves into activity.

We do it because after a period of rest, and especially when the rest follows spells of activity, the fascia of each muscle tends to contract. This tension – which can be severe after muscle spasms caused by cold or by bad posture – puts pressure on nerve fibres which can cause irritation or even pain – so the fascia has to be restretched to allow the muscle to relax fully.

Repeated use of any muscle through the sort of limited, unvarying range that a runner submits it to will make it increasingly hard and tense; the bigger the muscle becomes through training, the more it and its associated tendon come under tension. So a more elaborate programme of gentle stretching, to release this muscle tension, is advisable for all runners. If done properly it will produce many of the benefits of a relaxing massage – the soothed and smoothed-out feeling of relaxation.

The exercises should be done in the warm – they are best not attempted if the conditions are cold and you are unable to warm up thoroughly before you start. Too many runners have been injured by attempting incautious exercises before they have properly warmed up.

If you have a sedentary job it is worth cultivating the habit of stretching (simply, not the whole programme) after an hour or two of sitting. Students should stretch between classes and those who have to adopt rather fixed positions at work should stretch during lunch and tea breaks.

As we grow older, our natural suppleness is gradually reduced, and a good programme of stretching can do much to keep us supple, relaxed and comparatively free from tension.

'The trouble with stretching exercises is that they really are rather boring. I know that they have to be done, but I got so fed up years ago with doing them in sequence in a long session that I have now got into the habit of spreading them out through the day.

I may be sitting chatting to someone when for no apparent reason I'll get up and start trying to push the wall over – all I'm doing is exercising a calf muscle; or I'll find myself sitting watching television with my leg folded

Ⓐ

under me doing hurdling type exercises. It's far more practical, stretching like that, than by setting aside half an hour to go through the whole routine. And I find I can fit as much in during the day as I used to in a formal session. I think this is the reason those workout books and tapes have become so popular lately; people know they want to get fit and supple, but they *are* looking for a bit of flavour to keep the work interesting.

There are times, though, when these exercises have to be done in a concentrated sequence. Obviously before a race or before a fast training session I can't leave anything to chance – I've got to stretch all the muscles I might have to call on in a hurry. And in winter, too, I tend to do a lot of stretching before I leave the warmth of the house. Cold muscles are more at risk anyway, but there are added hazards in winter. I'm usually well wrapped up, which might make me slightly more awkward in my movements; and there's the danger of ice or mud underfoot – the body will automatically try to correct me if I slip, and there's always the danger of a groin strain or a muscle tear if I haven't stretched properly.

If you've never done these exercises before, don't rush them. If you're sensible you're going to be doing them from now on every day of your

running life, so there's no need to blaze away and try to get them all working perfectly at once. You'll probably feel stiff, even a bit sore, after your first few sessions. But don't worry, you can work through it, and the stiffness will soon go as your suppleness increases.

These few examples will help you with all the moving parts that running puts a strain on. In (A) you are easing the achilles tendon to greater flexibility, keeping the front foot flat and balancing with the back foot.

In (B) the calf muscle of the back leg (with the back foot flat on the ground) is getting the benefit. In both cases, change feet to give the same treatment to the other side. Do each exercise three times, and hold the position for 10–12 seconds each time to give the muscle a chance to stretch properly. Exercise (C) is for the lower back, the bottom quarter of the spine, and (D) is for hip mobility.

(E) and (F) both stretch the hamstrings (the former, of course, to be done with both legs outstretched in turn), and (F) also gives even greater flexibility to the lower back.

Finally, (G) is a really good all-round stretching and flexing movement. A lot of you will hardly be able to move forward at all to begin with, but in time you should be able to walk right up to your hands, even with palms and heels flat on the floor.

None of these is a jerky exercise. You should apply the pressure gradually in every case, hold each position for about 10 seconds, and gradually take the pressure off. Remember, you are *easing* your muscles into greater flexibility not snapping them into shape.'

The Running Machine

Now that you have decided that your goal is fitness, and that you are going to employ running as a means to that goal, it might be worth looking at just what is meant by 'physical fitness'.

Fred Wilt's *Run Run Run* gives a definition that we rather like. He defines fitness as 'the development of a body to a state or condition which permits the performance of a given amount of work, when desired, with minimum physical effort. The efficiency of physical effort depends upon the mutual development of the muscular, respiratory and circulatory systems.' This is a particularly useful description, because it introduces the idea of changing the state of the body.

If you are going to achieve physical fitness by running, you are going to have to run with sufficient intensity to produce significant physiological changes in your cardiovascular system (your heart, lungs and bloodstream) as well as in certain muscle groups; improved efficiency of the cardiovascular system is a basic requirement for all-round fitness. The effect of running on the muscle groups is rather more specific to running.

You are running to become and to remain fit, not to earn a Ph.D., and in attempting to explain the physical effect of running we do not propose to give a potted degree course in anatomy. Sports medicine and physiology are sciences, and a runner needs only to know enough to use them as a useful tool. It is more important for you to know where to go for information and advice than to try to turn yourself into an encyclopaedia of sports medicine, but it is as well if the runner can learn to cope with the occasional physical problems that might arise, and he will certainly have a better understanding of the complexities of the human body.

Training and the Body

Running for fitness will have a number of specific effects on the body; all will help you to run better and also, to a large extent, all will be beneficial to the efficiency and well-being of the body in general.

First, training brings about the enlargement of muscle fibres (not their number – that is determined at birth), giving them the power to work harder and more effectively, given an adequate supply of fuel.

Training will increase the number of the minute energy sources in the muscles – the *mitochondria* – which use the oxygen extracted from the blood to provide the energy needed for muscle contraction. More mitochondria will mean easier and faster fuelling of the muscles, which in turn means more efficient muscles.

This increased production of fuel will call for an increased supply of oxygen from the blood. To this end, a trained body will have an increased number of capillaries – the tiny vessels carrying the oxygenated blood to the muscles (tests have shown some 40 per cent more capillaries serving the thigh muscles of trained athletes than in the thighs of untrained subjects).

Finally, to meet this increased demand for oxygen, the heart-lung system will have to work harder and more efficiently. The heart, and the muscles which help the lungs to breathe deeply, will themselves grow extra capillaries and will work more efficiently, and your cardiac output will increase – the heart will need to beat less often to pump the same amount of blood around the body.

That, at its simplest, is what the walking, the jogging and finally the running will eventually do for you. The effect of running for fitness will be to produce a more efficient fuelling of the muscle mechanism for its task of moving the bones.

The Working Parts

It is quite possible to drive a car for your entire adult life without the faintest idea of what is going on under the bonnet. If, however, you take up motor racing, and need to get the best out of your car, you will quickly become obsessive about torque and gear ratios and anything which will contribute to the conversion of fuel into speed.

In just the same way a human, who is quite content in his pre-exercise existence as long as his body gets him adequately from place to place, tends to become fascinated by the working of this body once he is asking it to perform more efficiently. At top levels of competition this fascination, and what it reveals, becomes crucial to performance, but we felt that anyone determined to take the trouble to alter his or her body by running would welcome a more detailed summary of how a running body works, and why it works better as we get fitter.

The body is a machine, albeit a very complex and elegant one, and the Oxford Dictionary defines a machine as 'an apparatus in which the action of several parts is combined for the application of force to a purpose'. When we think of applying force, we usually think first of levers, and human levers are part of the skeleton.

The Bones

Our skeleton has two main functions. It provides a framework to protect the organs contained within it, and it provides points to which muscles can be attached, thus converting it to a machine for exerting force.

Our long bones in the limbs form the levers for lifting and locomotion, and our joints are the hinges and pivots of the machine; the levers themselves are held in place by the muscles and ligaments, and the whole frame is built on and around the spinal column.

Bones are beautifully constructed to give the best strength-to-weight ratio to suit their function. The short bones and some of the irregular bones are made to take compression but the long bones – the long levers of our arms and legs – are *hollow*, with a thicker wall in the middle, and they cope with a lot of bending and torsional stress as well as compression. They all contain bone marrow, which is the source of the blood cells.

Bones are strong, but stress is seldom applied to them simply. They are frequently subject to a combination of different forces – bending, twisting and compression at the same time – and they can quite easily be broken without any apparent impact. It only takes prolonged overuse, coupled with an imbalance of some sort, to effect a stress fracture.

An examination of the microstructure of bones reveals the special alignment of the bone substances to meet the forces imposed on them. Exercise maintains and improves this microstructure; inactivity reduces the strength and density of the bones. What we can do, by maintaining muscle tone and by the sensible choice of running shoes, is to protect them from unnecessary stress.

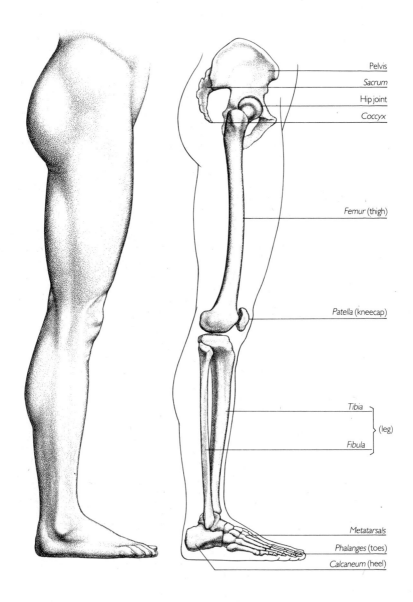

Pelvis
Sacrum
Hip joint
Coccyx

Femur (thigh)

Patella (kneecap)

Tibia
} (leg)
Fibula

Metatarsals
Phalanges (toes)
Calcaneum (heel)

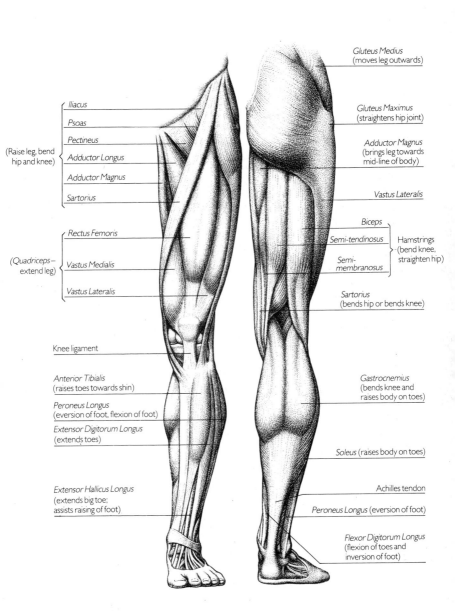

Gluteus Medius
(moves leg outwards)

Iliacus

Psoas

Pectineus

(Raise leg, bend
hip and knee)

Adductor Longus

Adductor Magnus

Sartorius

Gluteus Maximus
(straightens hip joint)

Adductor Magnus
(brings leg towards
mid-line of body)

Vastus Lateralis

Rectus Femoris

(Quadriceps –
extend leg)

Vastus Medialis

Vastus Lateralis

Biceps

Semi-tendinosus

Semi-
membranosus

Hamstrings
(bend knee,
straighten hip)

Sartorius
(bends hip or bends knee)

Knee ligament

Anterior Tibialis
(raises toes towards shin)

Peroneus Longus
(eversion of foot, flexion of foot)

Extensor Digitorum Longus
(extends toes)

Gastrocnemius
(bends knee and
raises body on toes)

Soleus (raises body on toes)

Extensor Hallicus Longus
(extends big toe;
assists raising of foot)

Achilles tendon

Peroneus Longus (eversion of foot)

Flexor Digitorum Longus
(flexion of toes and
inversion of foot)

The Muscles

Muscles are agents for moving things, and the skeletal muscles – the ones which move the long levers of our bones, are the ones that most concern the runner.

Skeletal muscle in the limbs is generally spindle-shaped – thickest in the middle and tapering at either end where it becomes tendon. Muscles are encased in tough, non-elastic membranes called *fasciae*, which not only surround them but also form part of their attachment to the bone. Muscles stretch and contract like elastic bands; tendons, which are tough, fibrous strands of varying thickness and form the cables linking muscles to the bone, stretch very little.

All skeletal muscles link two or more bones; they are anchored to the fibrous covering (*periosteum*) of these bones, generally with one tendon at the fixed end (known as the *origin*) and the other at the moving end (the *insertion*). Under certain conditions or injuries these endings can become detached.

Muscles cross the joint which they move – some cross more than one joint, and therefore produce movement in more than one place (the biceps, for example, which cross elbow and shoulder and cause flexion of both joints).

Mobility, then, is simply achieved by muscles contracting or relaxing, and so allowing the bones to move in the required direction. But not quite as simply as that. For the muscles achieve something every bit as vital as that – they *control* movement: depending on the signal they receive from the brain, the voluntary muscles – the ones that move when we want them to – can react either strongly or weakly.

As an example, bend your arm. The movement itself is pronounced, but the effort is minimal, and there is only the very slightest sensation of effort – even if the movement is done quite quickly. Now bend your arm again, but at the same time resist that bending by trying to keep it straight. You can still bend the arm at varying speeds, but also with as great an effort as you want to apply. Quite simply, the triceps, the muscle down the back of the arm, has been trying to restrain the biceps, the muscle in front, from doing its job. One muscle has been monitoring the action of the other, as it were by a paying out process.

This is the secret of any animal's ability to make the most subtle and refined movements: muscles involved in driving the body tend to work in pairs or in combinations, grouped round joints each having opposing actions. These muscles are known according to the movement they produce; every flexor muscle (for bending a joint) is opposed by an extensor (for straightening it); a supinator (turning upwards) by a pronator (turning downwards); an internal rotator by an external rotator, and so on.

Almost any physical action needs the combined movement of many pairs of muscles, and this action is known as muscle co-ordination. Even the act of standing still involves the use of muscles controlling the ankle, knee, hip, vertebral column, and head – a co-ordination that is very difficult, and takes a long time to master, but once learnt can be performed at will with ease and without thinking.

Muscles have other functions besides movement. With ligaments they hold the body together by helping to keep the joints in place. For example, the strength and condition of the knee joint depends very much upon the strength and tone of the quadriceps, the front thigh muscles. When a muscle is at rest it is still very slightly in tension. This tension and any slight movement generates heat, so that a good muscle condition – or muscle tone, as it is called – is important in both protecting the joints and in maintaining the body temperature. The effect of good muscle tone is particularly obvious in winter.

There are three kinds of muscle each with its own function and structure. We naturally tend to be most concerned about our *voluntary muscles* – those which remain under our conscious control. To these muscles the brain sends out signals via the central nervous system, and the muscles contract to order.

The *involuntary muscles* are not under our conscious control, but take their instructions from the autonomic nervous system. This system is concerned with regulating the automatic functions of the body, among them the heartbeat and the dilation and constriction of blood vessels; the automatic adjustment of their functions is very important, no more so than when we start running. When a conscious decision is taken to run, the autonomic system also becomes involved, automatically issuing special instructions to those parts of the system not under conscious control.

The *heart muscle* is a bit of an exception. While it is an involuntary muscle, it does have a somewhat similar micro-structure to the voluntary muscle, but it cannot sustain prolonged contraction.

The Vital Question

We are now going to get technical. In order to understand how running can help fitness, or why our diet might need changing, and why our cardiovascular system might need improving, we need to have a reasonably detailed answer to one simple question. How does a complex bundle of fibres try to pull its ends together and so move the working parts of our body?

Without going into photo-micrographs and a detailed study of electro-chemical reactions and the nature of enzymes and a description of the whole nervous system, this is roughly what happens.

Skeletal muscles, as we have seen, are wrapped in a sheath (fascia) and tapered at each end. Inside the outer sheath are bundles containing muscle fibres, each surrounded by a membrane (the *sarcolemma*). Each individual fibre is a round elongated single cell. Inside this cell are even thinner elements called myofibrils; these are the cell's contracting elements.

The myofibrils consist of two even smaller elements of protein – the larger is myosin, the smaller actin; and all these tiny filaments move in a fluid containing protein, glycogen and phosphates; this fluid reaches the muscle fibre through the sarcolemma and, in a two-way exchange system, waste products are carried away into the blood stream once the fuel in the fluid has been broken down.

It is believed that the muscle contracts when, on command from the brain, a temporary affinity of the myosin for the actin filaments causes each thin actin filament to slide over the thick myosin filament by means of a minute ratchet system. This action needs energy, and the energy demands fuel. In this case the fuel is adenosine triphosphate (ATP).

The continued replacement of this substance is absolutely necessary if we are to keep moving, and yet there is only a minimal amount of ATP present in the muscle at any given moment – enough to sustain contraction for just half a second before it needs to be replenished. When this is used up, a further five seconds' worth of fuel is found by breaking down another compound, CP (creatin phosphate) to produce more ATP. Then, when this is finished, some of the glycogen stored in the muscle is converted to ATP by a process called *anaerobic glycolysis*; this will keep us going at an intense level of activity for a full three-quarters of a minute.

Now that all the resources stored in the muscle have been used, the body has to think again – and call on a different system.

The Oxygen Process

Those first three steps in the muscle's use of its energy supply can all take place anaerobically – meaning 'without oxygen'. In these anaerobic processes, when chemical bonds are being broken down, by-products are created which – if they cannot be recycled or eliminated quickly enough – will build up, clog the system and eventually stop the muscle moving. When glycogen is broken down without the aid of oxygen to form ATP the process forms lactic acid as a byproduct, which so increases the level of acidity that the muscle cells cannot work. This is why neither you nor the best runners in the world can sprint flat out for, say, 400 metres before seizing up.

Any runner, trained or untrained, will breathe faster and deeper if he begins to run very quickly. He soon exhausts all the energy stored in his muscles, and his body is demanding an increased supply of the one substance that can now be used to enable the muscle to carry on continuous work – oxygen. You can carry stores of fuel, but the body cannot store oxygen.

The level at which you can maintain sustained work depends upon the amount of air you can get into and out of your lungs and the amount of oxygen you can extract from the air that you are breathing in. In fact one of the simplest guides to your progress towards fitness is how much longer it takes you to get out of breath when running at the same pace. It re-emphasises that the basis for all-round fitness is the improvement of the respiratory and cardiovascular systems.

The oxygen is carried round the body by the haemoglobin in the blood. In the muscle a substance is waiting called myoglobin, which has an even greater affinity for oxygen than has the haemoglobin; the haemoglobin readily yields up its oxygen to the myoglobin, picks up in turn the carbon dioxide which is the useless byproduct of the energy-making process, and takes it back to the lungs where it is breathed out.

Meanwhile, in the muscle, the process that allows long-distance runners to run long distances is taking place. It is called *aerobic glycolysis*, and involves the conversion of the muscle's glycogen, by means of the oxygen, into the ATP so necessary to sustain movement. This process takes place inside the mitochondria – tiny units (anything up to five thousand of them in a single cell) which produce the requisite enzymes, break down the proteins and the oxygen, and manufacture the necessary fuel for the muscle.

And, conveniently for all of us who want to see improvement in performance when we start running, mitochondria will grow in number when the muscles in the body begin regularly to demand more fuel.

The Blood Supply

This increased supply of fuel to the muscles, though, can be maintained only as long as the blood supply is increased. But the minute, fern-like capillaries at the end of the blood-line cannot cope – if they have been used to the comparatively leisurely blood flow of a sedentary individual – with a sudden increase in the demand for oxygen-rich blood.

They, too, will increase in number in a body in training, ensuring an easier flow of oxygen to the muscle cells; and at the same time, by the body's system of non-return valves and with some help from the contractions of the muscle itself, carry away the waste product, and CO_2 can be returned to the lungs more quickly and efficiently via the increased number of capillaries serving the veins.

This increased blood supply throughout the body is achieved in part, of course, by the heart simply beating faster, and in the early stages of fitness running this will be the only way that the heart meets the extra demand.

But in time your body will undergo the most important physiological change of all. Your heart will pump out more blood per beat than it did before – so your body will be getting the same blood with a heart beating slower . . . the machine will be, once again, operating more efficiently, and your pulse taken at rest will chart the improvement.

The heart, considered purely as a pump, generally has a low mechanical efficiency (estimated at only 10 per cent when at rest) so even the most modest increase in this efficiency can be seen as a large improvement.

For example, take an untrained person with a heart-rate at rest of 72 beats per minute. If, under a work load (say running) his rate increases to 180 beats per minute, this would theoretically increase his cardiac output two-and-a-half times. After proper training, though, his resting heart-rate would be as low as 40 beats per minute. So when he runs hard enough to increase his heart-rate to 180 beats per minute he is increasing his cardiac output four-and-a-half times – a dramatic 80 per cent improvement.

Not all this increased efficiency is felt by the skeletal muscles. The heart itself is a muscle and a non-stop muscle at that. It too will need extra capillaries to serve its own extra demand. And so too will the muscles which the lungs depend on. Extra blood coming round the body is no use unless it carries the vital oxygen with it, and the demand for extra oxygen means extra work for the lungs.

To fill our lungs with the air we need we increase the size of the thoracic cavity, the space inside our chest. While we are at rest, the diaphragm does most of this work, simply by raising and lowering itself and varying the available space; the movement is quite small – perhaps half an inch or so up and down – but deep breathing can increase its movement to three or four inches.

During hard exercise we are demanding even more air. Now the intercostal muscles will raise and lower the rib cage, thus further increasing the space in our chest, reducing the pressure inside and allowing the atmospheric pressure outside to force air in and inflate the lungs to their maximum. The very act of breathing itself, as we know, can become hard work, and indeed some 10 per cent of that increased supply of oxygen we are taking in is going to be used to fuel the breathing mechanism alone – most of it to overcome the natural resistance found in our air passages; no wonder, when we start breathing hard, we need to use our mouths as well as our noses.

Once the air is in the trachea, conducting airways divide and subdivide to conduct air to the minute alveoli – some three hundred and fifty million of them in each lung – from which the oxygen diffuses into the blood and through which the returning carbon dioxide is taken from the blood to be breathed out.

The cycle, then, is both ingenious and straightforward: air to the lungs, oxygen to the haemoglobin of the blood, blood pumped round the body by the heart to its farthest capillaries, haemoglobin transferring oxygen to the myoglobin of the muscles, mitochondria using that oxygen to synthesise ATP, muscles using the ATP as fuel and returning the waste carbon dioxide to the blood, capillaries returning carbon dioxide to the veins and back to the lungs, lungs breathing out the unwanted carbon dioxide and starting all over again.

In a body which has achieved any degree of fitness by running, the lungs will accept increased and continuous supplies of air without difficulty; the heart will pump more oxygen-rich blood through the body at every stroke; there will be more capillaries to carry the oxygen to the muscles; there will be more mitochondria to use the oxygen to fuel the muscle; and the muscle fibres themselves will be thicker and more tightly packed, and will thus contract with greater force.

A word about Smoking – Don't

The whole respiratory tract is an air filter. It starts by removing the largest dust particles in the nose where they are trapped by moisture or hair. In the airways in the lungs some of the surface area is cilliated. This means the surface cells have small hair-like whips which exert a non-stop concerted flailing action, a fast upward movement with a slow return. The whips are covered with a thin sticky mucus which holds any particle which falls on them; the mucus, and the rubbish it holds, moves steadily up the airways to the throat where it is either swallowed or spat out. This process can tolerate a lot, but cigarette smoke will slow it down, if not stop it altogether. In other words, smoking prevents our breathing machine from operating its own self-cleansing mechanism.

Furthermore, at the very end of the airways, inside the alveoli, another process occurs by which small scavengers called macrophages finally clear up and dispose of any unwanted matter at the very point where oxygen is taken into the blood. Again, smoking will impair this important function. So even if you don't believe lung cancer will happen to you, it is clear that smoking is actively working against your maintaining health and achieving the fitness you are running for.

So many people lead such sedentary lives that they will not notice the physiological effects of smoking until any real physical effort is required. Then the limiting effects of smoking are clearly felt. Depending upon the time elapsed between the last cigarette and the start of physical effort, for the same load smokers will have a heart rate which is ten to twenty beats per minute faster than that of non-smokers.

Smoking, too, will increase airway resistance two- or three-fold, thus multiplying the greater part of the effort of breathing. Again, if you are sitting slumped in a chair, with the lungs demanding very little air, this may not seem to matter. But when you are running, trying to meet the body's demand for oxygen, it becomes very important indeed.

The haemoglobin in our blood has an affinity for oxygen, but it has a far higher affinity for carbon monoxide. Smoke contains some 4 per cent carbon monoxide and since haemoglobin is naturally going to pick up the carbon monoxide first, the oxygen-carrying capacity of the blood is immediately reduced. This is the very opposite of the condition we require for enhanced fitness. Furthermore the body does not have any means of making up the deficiency during exercise or hard work. It is also worth considering that a concentration of 0.1 per cent or more of carbon monoxide in the air is highly toxic and would soon kill you.

Smoking tobacco was, is and always will be bad for you.

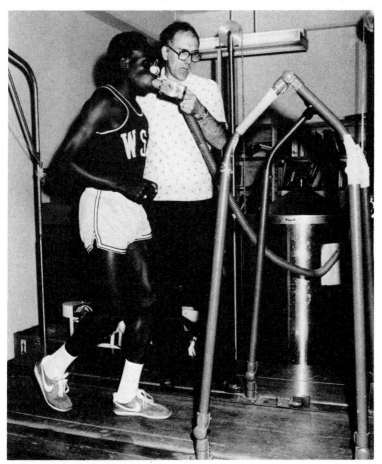

Looking under the bonnet: a test-bed
examination of the high-performance Henry Rono

Faster and Stronger

Now that the beginner is on the road, happy with the running he or she has undertaken, and perhaps aware already of some of the changes that it is beginning to bring about in the body, we can think about adding strength and distance and perhaps speed, too. From mere running, we are turning to something more like training.

Training means different things to different people. For many athletes it will be a means to a specific and very clear end – a particular race or an area championship. For others it will be the transition from a relaxed winter to a summer of active competition. To the newcomer, it might mean the eventual achievement of a best distance, or a personal best time on the local track – or just the further satisfaction of measurable progress. In a later chapter we will be looking at the question of training for a specific purpose. Here we can consider training in its most general terms – in increasing strength, in running more economically, in dressing properly, and so on.

The Basic Principles of Training

We have seen that running can produce changes in the body that will enable the body to work better. Training runners is an extension of that same theory – it involves changing their bodies sufficiently to improve their performance significantly.

If you apply a stress to the body, it will respond with an adaptation to that stress, so that it becomes capable of meeting the new demand. By carefully applying work loads, and allowing the proper recovery periods, the trainer will slowly and steadily raise the runner to a plateau of excellence beyond which the loading would become too severe and the runner would break down. This process calls for great care and subtlety on the part of the trainer – to maximise the runner's potential and yet avoid going over the top.

For most runners, operating at lower level and in most cases training themselves, the same principle applies. All runners, once moderately fit, will want to test themselves further; all will recognise the benefits of recovery periods – of hard and less hard training weeks; and all will know of, though few would be silly enough to put themselves at risk from, the dangers of seriously overdoing it – in their case indeed, it is likely that their bodies would rebel before they reached any danger point.

For the runner at the higher level, the trainer is now likely to apply the *principle of specificity*. This says that for the various tasks required from the body, there are exercises specific to that function. Curling with dumb-bells, for example, is specific to the biceps, swinging Indian clubs is not. As far as we are concerned, running is specific to running, soccer, though a perfectly good and enjoyable exercise, is not.

The application of this principle is further refined by applying different types of running training to improve the response of all the body's energy systems to their best advantage. Once again, runners at the top level are likely to use all the types of running described below – particularly those training for middle- and long-distance events.

Steady distance running: aerobic training, as we have seen in the previous chapter, can improve lungs, heart, and muscles for endurance work. The resting heart-rate will drop, the body will take in more air, and will take more oxygen from that air, and the network of blood vessels supplying blood to the muscles will increase.

Faster, interrupted running: known as interval training, this can powerfully stimulate the stroke-volume of the heart. It is not a method that should be used by the very young, or by those without an adequate background of distance work.

High-speed running: these sessions (anaerobic training) will eventually help to cope with these occasions when the byproducts of the muscles are creating conditions in the body which are unfavourable to further exertion.

Training schedules combining all three methods, and based on the general principles we began with, can be applied to any runner on an individual basis by a knowledgeable coach. All, too, in their way, can be of benefit to the fitness runner, though he or she is likely to lean far more on steady distance running, perhaps spiced with some interval training, than on the high-speed work.

'Making up the programme as you go along'
– a free-and-easy run through the streets of Sheffield

There is a fourth type of training discipline whose main virtue is that it is *not* discipline. It can be used equally well by fun runners, club athletes and international stars, and it has the thumbs-up from coaches and runners alike. Peter Coe explains:

'Fartlek is a Nordic word loosely translated as "speed play". It is an all-the-year-round component which allows the runner the freedom to choose his own variations.

Staleness is psychological, not physical. If it were physical athletes could not perform so well at the end of a hard season. In 1981 Seb progressed in July from a near world record 1500 metres in one country to breaking his own 1000 metres world record in another four days later. That was physically demanding. To follow this up with two world records in the mile a month later after six big meetings in between would have been the perfect recipe for physical staleness – if such a thing existed. Staleness is a loose word for being mentally jaded, and mental fatigue, whether caused by loss of concentration or through boredom, is at the root of staleness. Seb describes it best himself. "During and after such a season I was able to recharge my mental batteries with the refreshment of fartlek. I can do my own thing in my own way just as easily or as hard as I want to make it. Running round the lakes in Norway, or round the hills and parks of Sheffield, the refreshment of close contact with nature is invaluable."

This break from road and track – which can include a very hard session if you want it – is the great advantage of fartlek, and it is open to anyone at any level.

Fartlek is no more than varying the going in your time in your own way. Jog ten minutes, walk three minutes, run fifteen minutes, walk five minutes, sprint twenty seconds, jog three minutes, sprint fifteen seconds, run eight minutes, walk four minutes, run at a fast pace for three minutes, jog five minutes, run four minutes. That is an hour's training, and you can mix it up to suit yourself. Look at the trees, think your thoughts and come back feeling good; you write the programme as you go along.'

Now that we are running seriously, it is time to think seriously about what we are going to wear.

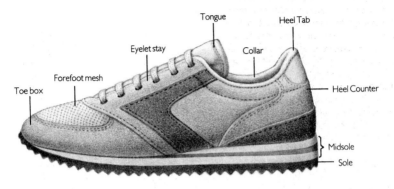

Shoes

Like building a house, a good place is to start from the bottom and where better for a runner to begin than with the feet.

There are no fewer than twenty-six bones in each foot, and these delicate structures have to withstand the considerable forces applied by the human body against the ground.

Running a seven-minute mile can mean 1000 foot strikes, and as each foot-fall has an impact of hundreds of pounds per square inch, 5000 strikes of this intensity in a five-mile run will be giving your feet a problem if they are not properly protected.

A comfortably-paced run lasting an hour is nothing special for most people after a period of training to this level. However, eight or nine thousand foot-strikes are likely to be something for the feet to complain about. Worse still, if the feet are not right to start with, any problems in that area will be reflected throughout a large part of the body, particularly in the knees.

First, before you start running, let's look for a moment at the state of your feet. The chances are that the more you use them the more you abuse them. There are very, very few shoes for everyday use that are not modified in some way because of style and fashion. There will be very, very few readers of this book who are not influenced by these factors. So even if you have chosen sensible shoes for your running, don't blame them for the trouble you may have stored up yourself by wearing shoes for every day that are orthopaedically damaging. Women are often prone to ankle swelling and strain when they start running. They have not done anything traumatic, they are just paying the price for high heels and narrow fittings.

But however badly you've been treating your feet in the past, your aim, now that you are running, must be to give them all the help they need.

If you are to extract the maximum pleasure and benefit from running, which also means avoiding overuse injuries, it is vital that you select the correct type of shoe for your particular needs. And getting the specification correct is not enough if it is followed up by careless fitting. Ideally every running-shoe shop would have trial shoes you could borrow in good condition in all makes, sizes and fittings for a trial. Since this is a non-existant Utopia, the final decision will be yours, and it should be made from the shoe specification and from how it feels on your foot. Here are a few points to remember:

1.   The toes must be free to spread, and the tips of the toes should not rub against the front of the shoe.
2.   When the shoes are laced, the space across the instep between the eyelets should be big enough for you to try more than one method of lacing, but not so wide that it diminishes support.
3.   Friction generates heat. Make sure that the fit that appeals to you does not permit rubbing. Blisters can form quickly.
4.   Wear the same size and type of socks for the fitting as the pair you intend to run in.
5.   If you are not sure into which class your foot-fall belongs, get another runner to observe for you. It requires a different design of shoe if you are a fore-foot or mid-foot striker from the type you need if you are a heel striker.
6.   Obtain guiding literature from the makers, or from the specialist running publications. The best is well written and informative. Buy from an interested sports shoe shop, preferably one run by runners for runners.

It is as well to study the basics of shoe design. If you are a heel striker you will need some 'meat' under the heel – not too spongy, but enough to be shock absorbent. Special inserts can help, but they often spoil the fit with a tendency to lift the heel too high out of the shoe (care must be taken about this, too, if lifting pads are fitted to ease achilles tendon trouble). A fore-foot or mid-foot striker needs the cushioning in the soles. For them heavy heels are no more than a dead weight.

Unless you are involved in serious racing, when you may need four or more different shoes for different surfaces, you will be well able to use one type of shoe for running on roads or grass. Track running, though, is different. At slow speeds most shoes will do, but at faster speeds, on cinders or shale, spikes will be necessary to obtain a safe grip. On synthetic tracks in dry weather a good road-racing flat is a good choice, but in the wet or at fast speeds, spikes again will be needed – not the same as cinder track spikes, but restricted in length – usually to about 5mm – by local track regulations.

These are general points that should set you on the way to a satisfactory pair of running shoes, but anyone preparing to pay the prices asked by shoe retailers today, or to choose between the dozens of models available, might find extra value in considering what the shoe of his choice should provide:

Protection: Since you will hammer the ground with your feet millions of times, you will want to protect them, particularly from the shock which will be transmitted to the rest of the body.

Support: The additional load placed upon the feet by running will strengthen the feet if it is slowly and carefully applied. But support for the intricate structure of the foot and its ligaments will be necessary, particularly when you start running for the first time. An important area of support is the heel counter which must be comfortable but rigid.

Flexibility: It is painful and causes stress to walk in stiff shoes, let alone run in them. The average runner will flex his shoes some thirty degrees, and if the shoe does not bend easily under the ball of the foot it will hurt. The upper shoe should allow for bending without the fold cutting into the foot. A shoe which is insufficiently flexible in the right place will throw painful stress on the calves and the achilles tendons.

Stability: A shoe must support the foot, but the cushioning effect of the shoes must not be so mushy that it throws too much sideways bending force on the ankle. This could be reflected in pain elsewhere in the lower leg.

Arch support: This is important, but its benefit can be negated if the shoe is cut away under the arch. This area of the shoe must be flat on the ground, otherwise it will tend to deflect or even collapse, making the interior build-up useless. No shoe with this defect is a good shoe. Flexibility in the fore-foot area is good but *not* in a distance shoe under the arch.

Wear: Shoes that are badly worn cause foot troubles. Since repairs are both expensive and time-consuming, a runner will be tempted to continue running on mis-shaped soles. He would be wrong to do so.

Midsole and sole formulation: This should be selected by manufacturers to give the characteristics they believe to be the most important. Do not choose shoes on price alone, or you will wind up with a pair of running shoes produced to cost rather than on good design.

Weight: A shoe's weight is quite secondary to the preceding requirements. Within reasonable limits, weight is of little significance except to racers. Leading shoe company research has shown that even in racing lighter is not necessarily faster – quality of the overall design is far more important.

Traction: Your shoe must provide a good grip, whatever surface you are running on. This can be obtained from soles that are ribbed, studded or cupped, or sometimes by a combination of any of these. A sole with a well designed and pronounced raised pattern has an additional advantage. It will not only give a good grip but by limiting the area in contact with road or track it will reduce the risk of overheating on hot surfaces. Fast running on tarmac or synthetic tracks in very warm weather creates a real problem in this respect. Make sure the pattern on the soles is not so widely spaced as to create local pressure points. On the other hand a well spaced raised pattern is worth looking for. Take care if you are running in marathon-type flat shoes in summer. The good are very good – the bad are blister-raisers. The light fast flats may seem attractive, but as with plimsoles and light tennis shoes, the soles may not offer enough protection from stones and small bumps. Bruises on the soles and particularly the heels must be avoided.

Uppers: These are very much a matter of horses for courses. Leather is heavier, and more so when wet, but it lasts longer and is cooler. Nylon is lighter, not so durable, and hotter. Different requirements may be best met by different materials and a wise combination of both is often the solution. A good nylon mesh, incidentally, makes for a better ventilated and cooler shoe.

The Tongue: This must take care of any point or line pressure from laces, it must be soft and cushioning and above all stay in its place and not wander down the foot when you are running.

Lacing: Eyelet arrangements that allow for a wide variety of lacing methods are important not only for snugness and support but also for relief. It is not uncommon to have the odd bump or knob on top of the instep, and to be able to arrange the laces so that this area is free from unwanted pressure is a big plus.

Inside the Shoe: To protect the toes a shoe should have a firm box, but this advantage can be spoiled if hard lines of stitching are left, or if there is too abrupt a change from firmness to flexibility. Always run your hand slowly and carefully around the inside of the shoe to feel for anything that could irritate after you have run a few miles.

Many insoles are now removable. This is a plus point, because frequently the insole is worn through at pressure points – behind the little toe, perhaps, or behind the big toe. These hollows are usually accompanied by some scuffing or wrinkling of the fabric covering of the insole – all potential trouble spots. But be sure that the removable insole stays in place and does not become a hazard by wrinkling or moving around. There is no point in improving hygiene if you are going to raise blisters.

Examine, too, the mid-foot region. Check that whatever method gives additional support to the saddle or arch bandage does not also leave an edge or a rib of stitching to cause discomfort later on.

Think very carefully and take *expert* orthopaedic advice if you are considering buying shoes that have a built-in correction for various foot abnormalities such as excess pronation (foot rolling when making contact with the ground). What might be ideal when exactly right could be very dangerous if wrongly chosen, and prescribing for the abnormal foot is not for amateurs.

A special note for runners who may not have experience of cross-country running but are intending to try their hand. Most runners will be taken up with the problems of studs versus waffles versus ripples, or whether spikes are possible on all sections of the course and how waterproof *are* these shoes? They will be overlooking a major hazard – *mud*. Those shoes that you thought were so snug and comfortable, the ones where you *had* to undo the laces to take them off, can change their nature completely in mud. The shoes may be waterproof, but mud changes many things. A foot in a puddle in some runs can leave your foot almost dry – but not mud.

You run down the slope to cross the stream and suddenly you are in mud. Over the top and down inside the shoes it goes. You now have a very slippery pair of extremities. Does your foot come out of the next mud patch cleanly? No it doesn't – the next thing you know you are groping around in mud looking for a shoe, or shoes, that have been sucked straight off your feet.

In the old days, when there tended to be much more 'plough' around the course and mud was more likely, there were several remedies: special shoes with a strap around the ankle was one; a section of motorcycle inner-tube, slipped over both shoe and foot, sometimes cut to fit round the ankle, was another. Seb's shoes had two eyelets punched into them, one on each side of the heel, and a soft tape threaded through them and tied in front of the ankle.

Beware of gimmicks: shoes over-cushioned around the ankle, for example or the enlarged heel tab claiming protection to the achilles tendon, which can cause unnecessary pressure and irritation.

Two final points on the subject of shoes: when you first buy a pair, especially if you are a beginner, just walk around in them at home for a while, to get their feel, before you set off for a run.

And last but not least, keep them in good condition and in good repair – badly worn shoes can bring on imbalance injuries, and imbalance injuries could stop you running.

Clothing

This is an area of great personal preference. If during the run you kept cool enough or warm enough and were always as comfortable as could be reasonably expected, then what you have been wearing is right for you.

There are some guidelines, though, and fashion is not one of them.

Cold Weather
Wind is the real enemy. A low temperature that is bearable on a calm day or night can become intolerable or even dangerous if the wind picks up. Athletes who run in climates that regularly have very cold winters, part of North America, for example, are well aware of this problem, and the wind-chill factor has a real meaning for them. The most important requirement for clothing in very cold conditions is that it should be wind-proof. Genuinely wind-proof outer garments will enable you significantly to reduce the total amount of clothing.

The light-hooded two-piece waterproof over-suits (track wetsuits) are ideal for this duty. The effect is to prevent the circulation of air and so keep in the heat, but remember that while you are keeping in the heat, you are also keeping in the moisture from perspiration. The best types of these waterproofs have well ventilated backs, and the newer materials claim greater permeability – that is they breathe more. While these waterproofs allow you to wear the minimum amount of clothes, what you do wear should be absorbent, and cotton is superior to synthetics for this purpose, though there are some new synthetic materials which are claimed to syphon off the moisture from the skin to the outside of the garment without the material staying damp. Wool is warm and absorbent, but it is easily felted and does not suit all skins.

If this type of waterproof clothing does not suit you, do not go to the other extreme and smother yourself in layer upon layer of gear. Remember, as a child you often ran about to keep warm, so realise that work done means heat released, and if you are overdressed you will soon overheat. Choose clothes that use the idea of small air pockets for insulation – they are warmer and lighter; the old World War Two commando string vests were very effective.

The Face

In intense cold a smear of protective oil or cream on the face is helpful, and in cross-country racing, where large areas of skin on the arms and legs are exposed, a smear of oil all over (even petroleum jelly on the inside of the thighs) is a good water-repellent. This prevents chapped skin, chafing or soreness from allowing the skin to soften. Although used in Scandinavia and North America, face coverings have not been a great success with most runners in Britain.

The Hands

If you have to run in gloves, then the lighter they are the better. Covered hands warm up quickly, and thick cosy gloves soon become a nuisance. Light wool or cotton gloves can be tucked away in a pocket, heavy ones cannot. Experienced winter runners often find that after a period of almost painful cold, hands warm up again and stay warm.

The Body

Most of your autumn running and even some winter running will need only a running vest and briefs or shorts under a fleece-lined tracksuit with perhaps a light sweater at most. Track suits should be of an easy fit, neither too snug nor too loose. The trousers are best straight or only slightly tapered, with long zips in the sides of the legs to facilitate pulling them on over your running shoes. Do not have elastic stirrups going under the foot. You may feel it is the style you like, but they are inclined to become uncomfortable and a nuisance.

The Head

In dry weather what you wear will depend upon how thick a head of hair you have and to what extent your ears are vulnerable to the cold. Some people develop painful headaches if their forehead gets too cold, but beginners soon become accustomed to the rigours of winter. Some runners are happy in a rainsuit hood, even with drawstrings around the face; others prefer a waterproof cap with a peak that protects from driving rain. Those with thin hair, or who want to limit heat loss from the head, may find a round knitted hat, which can be pulled down round the ears if necessary, the best protection. Balaclavas do seem to irritate around the face after a while.

Socks

Running is only pleasurable if your feet are happy, and the serious consideration they deserve does not end with your careful choice of shoes. Running feet are not short on circulation, as your extremities sometimes are at rest, but most people need warm socks when running in winter. Wool is warmest but it does not wear well; it also stretches and thus wrinkles very easily, and long woollen socks are inclined to slip down.

The best sock is a heavy cotton with a Terylene or nylon reinforcement. Those with a towelling type of foot and a cushioned sole are ideal. They keep their shape, they're very absorbent and they wear well.

Try to settle on a choice of socks and stick to them. It is important to know the socks you prefer running in and to have a pair with you when you choose your running shoes. Do remember that socks which are too tight will cause corns and will restrict circulation. Socks that are too loose will be uncomfortable, will wrinkle and will cause blisters.

Finally, unless you are lucky enough to have changing facilities at your place of work or study, your winter runs will be of the circular or out-and-home variety. In windy conditions start off into the wind, so that if you work up a good sweat it will not be so unpleasant on the way home. To get well warmed up – and thus damp – and then turn into a freezing wind is something to avoid.

Cold splash in the heat: a grilling marathon in Taiwan

Warm Weather

Choosing clothing for good weather is easy: a singlet or T-shirt and a pair of shorts. Headgear is slightly different; some hair styles require a headband which may also serve to absorb perspiration. In intense heat and glare you may favour a loose-fitting cap with the added protection of a peak. Whatever the type of headgear you choose, good ventilation is always important.

Running vests and shorts should never be too snug a fit, air circulating over the skin as freely as possible is important for adequate cooling. But also avoid the extreme of clothes so loose that they flap. They can cause chafing, particularly from baggy shorts, if you have to run in the rain.

Synthetic materials for summer wear do have advantages. Synthetic shorts do not become as waterlogged as cotton ones do. They are less apt to cling to the skin and they have the advantage of drying quickly.

Look for gear with seams that are as flat and smooth as possible. Even very small irritations not noticed at normal times are magnified a hundredfold when running.

The snug elasticated pants – they are hardly shorts – favoured by some women track athletes are not ideal for distance running, particularly in summer when they reduce cooling by restricting the free circulation of air.

Summer or winter, nearly all shorts and tracksuit bottoms are elasticated today. Be sure that the waistband is only tight enough to stay up; many athletes pull the waistline low on to the hips to avoid constriction when a draw-string support could be much more comfortable.

For those who wish to run in long socks, remember elastic restricts circulation. Soccer players use tapes, not elastic garters, a far better method in that tapes are adjustable to keep the garment in place, and no more. A little more trouble using tapes when dressing can avoid a lot of irritation on a run.

The Woman Runner

In general, advice on running gear is very much the same for women as for men, with the exception of the difficulties some women experience in finding a suitable bra for running, despite the increasing number of companies now producing sports bras.

Our experience in this area is a bit restricted, but it would perhaps be worth a woman asking herself, before she makes a choice, how much tolerance to active movement she builds up naturally at her work and at home. A job where she is continually reaching and pulling, say on a production line, is very different from one which involves sitting reading proofs. The large variety of shapes and sizes of women means that the best design solution could well be unique to each individual, and may, after some trial and error need a bit of high-class do-it-yourself to get the best results, particularly since what may be satisfying for the beginner may not necessarily work when distances increase.

Dry materials behave differently when they get moist from sweat; elastic constricts, fastenings can rub and cause sore spots. Would the increased use of Velcro help? We find it odd that while shoe manufacturers can supply reams of informative literature on product design, sportswear manufacturers are not doing the same for this essential piece of equipment – there must be many design improvements that could benefit serious women joggers and runners.

Looking good

Looking good often means feeling good and in most activities the best are always well turned out. If running gear is well chosen for its functional properties, then it only needs to be kept clean to look right.

Fashion sportswear has become deeply entrenched in sports like tennis and soccer, and it has now arrived in running. There are only two criteria that matter when choosing running gear: Is it suitable for its purpose, and does it fit? Club colours can add a touch of brightness if that is what you want, but the old grey sweatsuits – to which Seb is addicted – are above all functional.

If you find you need a sweatband, use one. If you find a wristband is useful to wipe away sweat, use one, but don't buy them because they look pretty. For all the peripheral gear, the recommendation is try it before you buy it, borrow it if necessary. The last thing a sensible runner needs, whether in competition or running for fitness, is a case of the cycling disease where large sums of money change hands for minutely modified equipment in the belief that it will make you go further and faster.

The ventilation on wet weather running gear is more important than the colour, and zips in the legs, long enough to ensure they slip easily over running shoes, is more important than stripes or coloured panels.

Strength Exercise

Training for running is not solely running. To increase all-round strength as the running becomes more demanding, as well as simply to make a change in the fitness routine, there is considerable benefit in introducing yourself to a series of exercises.

For runners there are two kinds of strengthening exercise. The first group is for the development of explosive strength – for sprinters, jumpers, throwers and the like; these are usually performed using free weights or a multi-gym, and in most cases they are geared towards the development of a specific muscle or muscle group.

The other type is used for developing all-round strength with endurance, and is also a general conditioner – and it is these exercises – used singly or in sequence – that are more likely to concern the fitness runner.

When the various exercises in this group are performed continuously in a series of sets, with prescribed intervals between sets, we have the basis of circuit training. The variables here are the number of different exercises in a circuit, the number of repetitions in each set, and the recovery time between each set. A further variable for the really tough is the number of circuits that can be completed. An additional refinement is placing a time limit on a given number of repetitions and an overall time for a full circuit.

Circuit training is best done in a gymnasium or a sports hall where you can move easily from one exercise to another, each already set up in its own area. But it is quite easy to select exercises which can be done separately, or in pairs or threes, in the home, which is probably the best way for beginners to start. Your local authority will know if any of the schools have gymnasium facilities open on any evening in the week, or whether there are any evening institutes or polytechnics with classes suitable for your strength and circuit training. This aspect of your training can often seem attractive in itself, and it is good practice not only to have a rest day each week, even when you have become well adjusted to running, but to do an evening's strengthening exercise as a complete change from running.

Weight training is a specialised form of exercise, and we would advise you to seek expert advice before you start, and only to use weights under supervision at first. The gymnasium exercises, though, can be performed alone, or by people in pairs, after some preliminary description and explanation.

'With all these exercises, begin gradually, and build up the number of repetitions and/or sets of repetitions to meet your own fitness targets. The depth jumping and bounding are called plyometric exercises, and require extra care when attempted for the first time.

Depth Jumping To develop elastic strength – the strength involving contractile and stretch components in movements done at speed and under load. A useful exercise for developing sprinting speed and fast uphill running. To avoid injury, keep both feet together at all stages. Pause slightly at the top of each box, the first of which should be slightly lower than the others in the sequence.

Burpees A combination of squat thrusts and vertical jumps to condition the gluteal and quadriceps muscles and to develop dynamic strength. The legs should extend fully backwards, and in the recovery the feet should return close to the hands to obtain a good jumping position. The best results come when the whole exercise is performed as quickly as possible.

Beam Jumps Start with the beam within reach of the arms with the feet on the floor. Later an even more helpful effect is achieved by progressing to a beam height which requires a jump to reach it. Combine the spring and the follow-through in one smooth, continuous movement. A good exercise for co-ordination, dynamic leg strength and upper-body development.

Bench Step-ups Select a box or a bench that will raise the thigh to the horizontal. Raise the body, not too slowly but without jerking, by lifting on the bent leg. Do not use the other leg to assist take-off. Alternate with an equal number of repetitions on each leg. A good strength endurance exercise, but the repetitions should be built up cautiously.

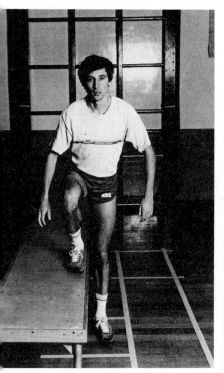 

Inclined Press-ups These increase the load on the arms and are a progression from ordinary press-ups. They are tough on triceps and pectoral muscles. All press-ups are a good all-round torso toughener, though older exercisers should approach them with caution. Hold the head in line with the back, and keep the back straight. Lower the face to within two inches of the floor.

Bounding Like depth jumping, this exercise develops dynamic leg strength, but it places a greater load on the ankles. Progress carefully. A useful variation is hopping on one leg then the other. Increase the severity either by longer repetitions or by bounding uphill. Or try reducing the number of bounds or hops required to cover a fixed distance.

Leg Raisers To strengthen abdominal muscles. In this exercise the legs should be kept straight and raised slowly to at least mid-way (i.e. at right angles to the body). This spin off, by which the exercise is done hanging from the wall bar, is excellent. During this phase the spine is fully stretched, which helps problems of tension and postural defects.'

	Gymnasium circuits					
Total time elapsed (minutes)	**Exercise**	**Duration**	**Recovery**	**Repetitions per set**	**Recovery between sets**	**Number of sets**
	Run to gymnasium, or start with warm-up run	1-2 miles				
10	Extra warm-up and loosening	10 minutes				
30	Static stretching exercises	20 minutes				
55	Leg raising, from wall-bars	20 seconds	20 seconds	5-12	2 min	2-3
59	Depth jumping from boxes [progressing, with more boxes, to]	20 seconds [60 sec]	30 seconds [60 sec]	1 [1]	2 min [2 min]	3 [2]
64	Bounding	5 minutes				1
69	More stretching exercises	5 minutes				1
70	Sit-ups	1 minute		30-60		1
75	Rope-climbing	5 minutes				1
77	Beam-jumping and pull-ups			5	1½ min	2-3
81	Scissoring (hanging from beam with legs raised – rotating pelvis and crossing legs while keeping legs straight)	10 seconds		1	3 min	2
83	Back strengthening (lying on stomach, arching back)	10 seconds	10 seconds	6		1
84	Press-ups with feet raised			25		1
88	Step-ups on box or beam (with or without weights)	until tired				
	Stretching after each circuit	10 minutes				

The Stronger Runner

With increased confidence from longer running sessions, and perhaps with some extra strength gained from work in the gymnasium too, the runner is going to be looking for other ways of improving both his speed and his endurance. Three types of training we would recommend all tackle the problem in a different way, but all play their part in improving the performance of your body.

Interval Training
This is probably the most common type of running training attempted when the conventional steady long distance running has given all the early benefit that it can offer.

The principle of interval training is that of spaced work. A work load is applied, generally from thirty to forty seconds, which speeds up the heart. This is followed by a recovery period. The subsequent intervals of work and recovery periods are adjusted in duration and number to suit the athlete and the level of training reached.

The duration and intensity of the work should be sufficient to raise the heart rate to a target time, and the recovery period long enough to allow the pulse rate to fall to the threshold rate at which the work interval should recommence. As a rough guide add 20 per cent to your best time for the distance run, and allow a recovery time which is three times longer than the running time.

The aim of this type of training is to increase the volume of blood pumped by each heartbeat. The underlying idea is that when the work load ceases and the muscles are recovering, the powerfully stimulated heart continues to fill and pump at almost the same level as during the working phase. The end effect is to achieve a greater dilation of the heart, and indeed very big increases in stroke volume have been recorded at the end of three or even two months.

Among the experts there is some divergence of opinion on the effectiveness of interval work. The pro-interval coaches claim it is a more effective method than steady distance running to increase cardiac output and oxygen uptake. The pro-steady running camp argues on the other hand, that the effect it achieves is more transient, and that to consolidate the base of your training steady running is best.

We use both methods in our training but regular interval training does not start until March.

In East Germany interval training is restricted to those over fourteen years of age.

The application of interval training has to be done very carefully and we would emphasise that the schedules need to be specific to the individual and his current condition.

Its plus point is that an athlete can undertake a lot more fast work in a short period because the lactate levels in blood do not become intolerable. It is also a rapid way to become used to fast work, and even if the development of the heart is not the main aim we find it has a specific role between steady running and speed endurance training.

The recovery period is variously prescribed as a rest or walk/jog recovery. An important factor in the choice is the weather (if it is cold or damp, then jog) and/or the feelings of the athlete. Some runners doing fast work tighten up even in short rest periods, and they would be better off keeping on the move and jogging in the recovery period.

It would be unwise to use this method as the main plank of training for fast middle-distance work because the lactic acid level in the blood does not reach the levels obtained by hard speed endurance training, which would use runs of two minutes or more with short recoveries. The latter is much closer to actual race conditions and to the lactate levels that will be experienced.

But we have found a special use for interval training. If Seb has been out of normal training through injury (*not* illness) and has managed to keep active by way of swimming or cycling or both, then after only a little steady running a few sessions of interval training, say 12 x 200 metres, increasing to 20 x 200 metres, soon brings back some snap and speed into his work. Provided the training base and his condition is sound, it provides us with a rapid return to near form.

We repeat that it is *not* recommended for a fast return to form after illness, because it is all too easy to overstimulate the heart.

Later in this chapter we make some suggestions for newcomers to interval training and speed-endurance running on how to go about planning their training sessions.

Speed-endurance Training

The old adage that speed kills is certainly true. Quite a few people find they can run quickly, and many will find that after some distance training they can keep going quite comfortably for a few miles. But ask any of them to run very quickly for only half a mile, and they will soon be in trouble.

If we think of speed endurance training as having two complementary meanings then we can understand the training better. It is making endurance running faster by learning how to endure speed.

Maintaining speed causes you to use more oxygen than you can extract from the air. You rely on the immediate release of energy in the muscles, which is soon spent. The by-products of this energy-release build up in the body, and the alkaline buffers in the blood cannot take up any more acid. In the end, which comes all too quickly, the whole machine stops through exhaustion.

Here psychological factors are important. Not only does the body have to learn how to delay this process, but the mind has to learn how to force the body to continue functioning while the brain is continually receiving signals to stop. For certainly the body can continue working longer than you think, painful though it may be.

This type of training, more than any other, requires careful assessment of the proper recovery period – not just the rest between runs, but the intensity of the training on the next one or even two days. Speed endurance is the most stress-inducing of all the training methods and can be destructive if over-used. Athletes refer to its misuse as a 'breaking down', as opposed to a 'building up' which is the real aim of training.

Speed endurance training consists principally of repeated extended high speed runs. The distances used are usually 600 metres, 800 metres, 1000 metres and 1200 metres. The best effect is obtained from running with an effort of 95 per cent or better.

Only experience can teach the coach and athlete how best these sessions can be applied but the following simple mistake should not be made. Do not think that the total distance of a set of runs gives the same effect regardless of the length of the run. For instance, if the proper recovery times are observed 8 x 600 metres is not as hard as 6 x 800 metres, and 4 x 1200 metres is harder still. The 4800 metres run is the same distance in each case, the effect is not.

Learning to cope with these runs with a recovery time of twice the running time (when running 1200 metres, recovery is only the same time as the run itself) is very hard, but it is a vital piece of training for all runners for racing between 800 metres and 5000 metres, or even up to 10,000 metres.

Maintaining an even pace is the most economical way of running any race above 400 metres, but in practice there will always be the moment when however, tired you are, you will want to produce a sustained burst. This type of training will help you to meet that requirement.

Resistance Running

This comes in many forms, but only two are relevant here; both involve hill running.

Running up inclines is hard work and is good for style, since the arm action is more vigorous and a higher knee-lift is required. Sessions of running up steep hills, preferably with inclines of one in six or more, is a great conditioner but the first few sessions should be approached with caution.

The most testing form of hill running is up long steep sandhills, which calls for the most pronounced, laboured exaggeration of running movements. Pulling the feet out of the sand, lifting the knees even higher and driving the arms extra hard is exceptionally tiring. Sandhill running is also the most searching. It seeks out any weakness anywhere, and the calf muscles and the achilles tendons get severely worked.

These sessions must be approached with the greatest caution. If you have access to such an area where this work can be carefully incorporated into a regular schedule, well and good, but it is unwise to approach this kind of training on a one-off basis without slow familiarisation. Don't go on holiday, look for long high sand dunes and have a hard workout. The chances are you will limp around miserably for the rest of your stay.

Easing into Session Training

Interval training will be quite new to most runners, and like all first-time training it must start slowly and be progressively increased. We would recommend one session a week for the first month before incorporating any speed endurance into the programme. In any case, two sessions per week of interval training will meet the needs of most runners.

Repetitions of 200 metres is not the only programme used. Runs up to 400 metres are quite common, but 200-metre repetitions are easier to handle when you first start.

Warm up carefully – don't forget your stretching – and start off with a set of ten runs. Keep to sets of ten until any soreness or stiffness which may have resulted from these runs has disappeared. If your first set of ten does not cause any problems, progress to sets of fifteen runs, and so on. For a distance runner we would suggest lengthening the sets of runs up to about thirty runs per set rather than reaching twenty runs per set and then increasing the speed of the run, which is a possible variant. Rather than increase the speed, the distance man could decrease the recovery time.

Once you have managed a few sets of 20 x 200 metres, we would expect you to find it easier to maintain a faster steady pace on the road.

Speed Endurance: again, for the general type of runner, we would recommend lengthening the sessions to 1000 metres or six-tenths of a mile before increasing the speed of the 600-metre or 800-metre runs. Also at this distance it is still better to cut the recovery time rather than to increase the speed of the 1000-metre run.

All the time, remember to check your pace judgment and keep looking at your watch. As with interval training, these sessions will improve your steady running speed.

Putting on the Style

Everybody runs in a different way, and most runners, unless they are reaching for the heights, are unlikely to modify their style very much. Activities depending upon fluent movement, like ballet and gymnastics as well as running, need the faults ironed out very early on, and the correct movements practised as soon as possible. At some stage it becomes too late to start correcting ingrained faults, and for older fitness runners correction becomes so difficult that there is a danger of it becoming counter-productive. But this does not mean that style is not important in running, or that it is not worth examining the running body in detail.

In engineering, particularly on the design side, there is an old saying that goes like this: 'If it looks right, it very likely is. If it looks wrong, it certainly is.' This is equally true of running style. A good style does not guarantee that you are a great runner but a bad style almost certainly guarantees that you are not. There will always be a few exceptions to this rule, but not many.

Imperfections in some areas, of course, are not as important as others. Anyone who remembers Zatopek might argue that style can not be all that important. The answer to this is that Zatopek would certainly have been an even better runner without the gross waste of energy caused by his tight arm action and the agonised head-wagging. That the whole is greater than the sum of the parts is never more true than of style.

There is a magic about the all-together athlete, a beautifully balanced pouring-out of well concealed effort. Good style and efficient movement are inseparable. Starting at the head and finishing with the feet these are the key factors:

Head
This should be well poised on the shoulders – not too far back, as in exaggerated effort – this restricts breathing and at the same time causes the stride to shorten.

Keep it still, the head must not turn. Running head down also restricts breathing, and as the head is a heavy weight, it will alter the line of carriage just to balance the body.

Neck
A well poised head is easier to balance, therefore the muscles have less work to do and neck strain is considerably lessened. Neck strain soon shows with the sterno-mastoid muscles standing out like tight cords. Remember, neck strain does not contribute to forward propulsion.

Shoulders
'To every force there is an equal and opposite reaction.' In high speed running one depends more on the reaction of the arms to offset the drive of the legs, and when you are running with a fast cadence, contra-rotation of the shoulders to any degree is hardly possible. Whenever the fast runner is tiring, though, he starts to labour and roll the shoulders, but at slower speeds some contra-rotation is natural because the arms cannot move with as much vigour. Again, this must not be excessive. Overstriding, which is mechanically inefficient anyway, will tend to distort shoulder movement. While running do not stick out the chest by forcing back the shoulders – it creates tension, which means wasted energy.

Arms
A very essential part of running. Upper-arm development is important to all runners. Sprinters need good muscular development to provide the mass for the reaction to the powerful leg drive required for their event. Middle-distance runners have to attack hills, which requires a good knee-lift and a vigorous arm action. Long-distance runners require endurance-toughened arms that do not drop with fatigue. At any cross-country event, and on hilly sections of long runs, you can hear the old parrot-cry 'use your arms' or 'drive with your arms' often directed at schoolboys and attenuated ectomorphs who have neon-tubes for arms. The under-trained and/or under-equipped can often be seen dropping their arms from the sheer fatigue of maintaining the arm position and action.

Steady fast running requires a vigorous action with the elbow *unlocked*. The angle between upper and lower arm should be about ninety degrees, but not with the elbow locked. During the backward motion the arm should be slightly extended, and then slightly flexed to something less than ninety degrees on the return.

The carriage of the arm should be low, for two reasons. First, it is less strain on the shoulders if the arms swing close to the body with the upper arm hanging more or less vertically, and the elbows in rather than sticking out spikily. Secondly, arms cannot be lifted into the driving position if they are already there. In the driving position the arms are best moved in a plane parallel to your direction (the sagittal plane) but in distance running, with its far less robust action, the arms will want to swing slightly across the body.

A clenched, high arm action is more tiring and mechanically does not provide the same reaction as the lower arm carriage. The wrists should be loose (though without the hands flapping wildly), fingers should be relaxed, usually with a light curl and with the thumb resting lightly on the index finger. Clenched fists betray unnecessary strain.

Hips
The part played by hips is not readily seen except through the general carriage of the runner, and especially in his stride length. When runners lack flexibility in the hips they often attempt to attain a good stride length by increasing the forward lean of the body. This tends to be self-defeating, because it hinders front knee lift and toe-off comes earlier. While some rotation takes place, the accentuated hip rotation cultivated by the race walker is not desirable in a runner. It often shows as an exaggerated roll as a runner reaches for stride length, especially when tiredness sets in.

Knees
Seen from the front the knees should not describe a circle, but should move in an arc parallel to the sagittal plane. In an all-out drive in flat-out running, or when attacking a hill, the knees should allow the leg to straighten fully in the driving phase. A good knee-lift is an economical way of preserving stride length. It increases the flinging effect of the loose-hanging lower leg so that it flicks forward easily but not too far at the end of the recovery phase. If the leg is fully straightened, at this stage, it throws a stress on the knee joint as the leg snaps out straight, and the runner over-strides. Over-striding places the foot strike too far in front of the centre of gravity of the body. This has a retarding effect, tends to promote a heavy heel-strike and unnecessarily jars the body.

Knees should also allow for a high heel lift of the swinging leg – the faster one runs, the higher the heels. When the heel is tucked up close to the buttock the leg is folded into half its length and this brings the centre of gravity of the leg closer to the pivot point, which is the hip joint. Now the leg is a much shorter lever, and the effort required to swing the leg forward to take up the supporting phase is much reduced. Further, when the heel is dropped it falls freely under gravity and being free to swing is easily flung forward without effort. Remember, good style promotes efficiency.

Ankles
The requirements of the ankle exemplify the basic requirements of all athletic endeavour: strength with flexibility. The ankle is at the receiving end of heavy loads with shock, tension and bending combined. The ankle must be strong to cope with uneven ground, with slipping or with any other accident, but in the context of style our main concern is with flexibility, because of the effect it has on stride length.

When the foot hits the ground the ideal foot-strike is the one that makes contact first with the ball of the foot but allows the heel to lower and kiss the ground immediately after the touchdown, when the leg is then in the supporting phase, slightly bent at the knee. Meanwhile the body is continuing to move forward so that the runner with the greatest range of movement in the ankle will be the one who can leave the foot in *flat* contact with the ground the longest.

This delays toe-off to the very last moment and extends the duration of the driving phase in which the very powerful calf muscles can contract and contribute to forward propulsion rather than pushing the body upwards.

The fault of over-striding has been emphasised. It is in the driving phase where stride length is effectively increased.

Toe-off
By this we mean that as the heel begins to lift it should be driven by the forceful contraction of the calf muscles, rather than just being a foot lifted off the ground. This drive should be continued right through to the toes, which should maintain driving contact until the very last moment. Place the foot flat on the ground and note the position of the ankle bone by placing it in line with the leg of a chair or table. Then still leaving this foot *flat* on the ground take a stride forward. See how far you can stride with the stationary heel still in contact with the ground.

As soon as you feel the tightness in front of the ankle or in the calf you will realise that with more flexibility the stride could be longer. Now slowly raise the heel from the ground and the ankle bone will lift and move forward. Continue this movement until the ball of the foot is off the ground and only the toes are in contact. The distance the ankle bone has moved horizontally from the chair leg is the distance you have added to your stride. Since this also depends upon the range of movement allowed by your ankle it is easy to see the contribution to your stride that ankle flexibility provides.

Feet
When running, feet seldom make contact with the ground in such a way that a line drawn across the ball of the foot makes instant contact along its whole length. The side of the foot is the first point to touch, after which the foot rolls to flat contact with the ground. This is called pronation, and is only safe and allowable over a limited range. There is a considerable risk in distance running from excessive pronation, and here prevention is much better than cure. Orthotics – inserts in the shoes – may be necessary.

The Body as a Whole
Generally, seen front on, a runner should progress in a straight line with the knees moving smoothly in a vertical plane and not seen to move in and out across the body. The heels, too, should not be seen to move inwards during the toe-off. It is, in fact, often seen in an exaggerated form with some sprinters during the start and early acceleration – and it is wasteful. Style is not merely a matter of aesthetics, it is harmonising a series of separate movements into a single economical effective motion.

Seen from the side, the main features we would look for would be: head well poised, trunk either erect or with just the slightest forward lean, arms held easily, hands and neck relaxed, a clean knee lift, good foot plant, with the knee nicely bent on contact *under* the centre of gravity (or just a few inches in front) and generally a smooth flow. Even the casual and uninformed observer seems to have an immediate appreciation of a smooth, elegant, purposeful and effective style. Remember, once again, 'if it looks right, it very likely is – if it looks wrong, it certainly is.'

The Critical Eye

Point by point Peter Coe, coach, analyses the style of Seb Coe, runner.

1 & 2 The head well poised avoids the neck straining to carry an off-balance load.
3 Leading shoulder without excessive contra-rotation.
4 Shoulders neither hunched forward with a pinched chest, nor forced back with out-thrust chest which would cause tension in the back.
5 Upper arm hanging naturally, elbows in. The arm moving forward is flexed to 90 degrees.
6 The other arm has 'unlocked' the elbow and is straightening as it moves backwards.
7 In steady pace running the hand may move comfortably slightly across the body.
8 Unclenched fingers, hands and fingers loosely carried, well relaxed.
9 Lead leg nearly straight (*never* lock out.)

10 Good heel lift – not as much as in sprinting, but enough to produce a forward fling.

11 This is important. The leading foot has slowed and has nearly stopped moving forward relative to the ground. The knee will start bending and the foot will touch the ground without any forward motion and will have dropped so that the strike is on the ball of the foot and the heel contact following on very close to first contact.

Still photographs are deceptive – it would appear from this one that the heel will strike first – but it will not. Some runners *are* heel strikers, though, and the shock on the achilles tendon and the spine is proportional to the degree to which the heel takes the load rather than the forefoot.

N.B. Not a style point, but an important one: note the use of the crown of the road rather than the camber, to avoid the danger of imbalance injury.

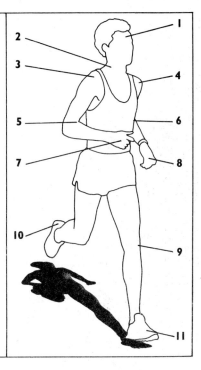

Fuelling the Machine

Fitness cannot be achieved solely by exercise. Even if the machine is made more efficient by running, and consequently works better, most of the fuel – all except the oxygen, in fact – is obtained by eating. The condition of your body, however well you train, will be determined to an important degree by how much you eat, and by what you eat. In short, if you want to keep your body in shape, running is not a substitute for dieting. On the other hand, diet, and some knowledge of nutrition, can be of real help to the runner.

Digestion

For our purposes the digestive system is not treated in any great depth because it is not 'trainable' in the sense that other components of fitness are. We are concerned with food only as a source of energy and growth, though the way the digestive system processes certain foods will influence our diet and, on the practical level, the time at which we eat and train.

We need food as fuel to burn for energy, and also, after we have reduced and reassembled it, as the building material for growth and maintenance of the body. In addition, it has to supply those essential ingredients which the body cannot synthesise for itself.

The greater part of the human body is water, about 60 per cent in males and 50 per cent in females (fat contains only a little water, and women normally have a higher percentage of fat than men). Water is composed entirely of hydrogen and oxygen, so 99 per cent of our body consists of hydrogen, oxygen, carbon, calcium and phosphorous. The remaining one per cent is mainly sodium, potassium, iron, magnesium, chlorine and sulphur, plus a few trace elements.

Our principal foods are proteins, carbohydrates and fats – protein mainly for tissue replacement (protein makes up approximately 12 per cent of the human body); carbohydrate as the quick source of energy, in that it is quickly burned as a fuel; fat as the most convenient way energy can be stored and as protection for the body.

Proteins are compounds of nitrogen, carbon, hydrogen and oxygen, together with essential minerals. A molecule of protein is made up of hundreds of molecules of amino acids. Most of the amino acids can be synthesised in the body, but those that cannot, the essential ones, must be contained in the diet, and animal proteins are a better source of these than vegetable proteins. Proteins are also the only source of nitrogen for the body.

Protein which is surplus to the requirements of body maintenance is converted to glucose and burned off as fuel, but if our diet is deficient in energy foods the protein will be consumed for energy; if this condition is prolonged the body will be robbed of replacement material and muscle wastage will occur which, if continued, will ultimately result in death.

With the best balance of essential amino acids as the criterion, the following foods are ranked in order of merit: eggs 100 per cent; fish, meat 70 per cent; soya beans 69 per cent; milk 60 per cent; rice 56 per cent; corn 41 per cent.

Carbohydrates are simpler compounds, containing only carbon, hydrogen and oxygen. They are the quick energy foods in that they can be metabolised faster.

Carbohydrates are taken in simple form as sugars or in more complex form as starches; starchy foods such as potatoes, pasta and bread also represent the cheapest of the energy foods.

The speed at which they can be digested must be considered when planning pre-exercise meals; unlike fats they can pass through the stomach quickly.

Carbohydrates, when converted to glycogen, can be stored in the liver and the muscles, but only in a very limited quantity, enough perhaps for one inactive day. Carbohydrate does not supply any of the essentials that the body cannot synthesise, and any surplus is quickly deposited as unwanted fat. Unfortunately carbohydrates are the main ingredients of the sweet and tasty foods and confectionaries.

Fat is generally held to be the villain in the diet war, but even though the average diet contains too much fat it is still necessary for its essential fatty acids and, because some of our necessary vitamins are fat soluble, a fat-free diet would lack these. Fat also yields twice as much energy as protein or carbohydrate, and can therefore save meals from being too bulky.

Nevertheless, more oxygen is required to reduce fat, which is a serious consideration for a runner. And although fat feels more comfortable to eat, and stops you feeling hungry too quickly after a meal, it stays longer in the stomach and so delays the start of serious exercise or heavy exertion.

It is slightly inconvenient that whereas animal protein is the best source of essential amino acids, vegetable fats are the best source for the essential fatty acids, the absence of which might lead to damage of the arteries by allowing excess quantities of cholesterol to accumulate.

The fatty acids themselves come in several forms, which will be familiar, if only in name, to those who have seen cholesterol climb high in the unpopularity ratings in the last few years. A *saturated* fatty acid is one which has taken up all the hydrogen atoms it can; an *unsaturated* fatty acid is one that has not. The former are found as solid animal fats such as butter and lard, the latter are more often liquid vegetable oils. A further division exists in the unsaturated fats between mono- and poly-unsaturated types; it is the latter that is lowest in cholesterol. In this respect margarine is better than butter, but it is still a matter for selection, as some brands of margarines have a far higher content of animal fat and thus more undesirable mono-unsaturated fats than others.

Vitamins are essentials that the body does not have the enzymes to synthesise. An all-round balanced diet will contain all the necessary vitamins for well-being, so that additional vitamin supplements should not be needed. Only the smallest amounts of the vitamins are required for normal health, and while the excess intake of most vitamins can easily be eliminated by the body, too much vitamin A or D could be harmful, since they are fat-soluble and can therefore build up in the body. A vitamin deficiency could possibly arise from the way the food has been stored or prepared. Overcooking or boiling, or even the wrong storage of fruit or orange juice, could destroy sufficient vitamin C to make the diet an inadequate source, but this would be unlikely in practice. It is rare, certainly in this country, to see obvious symptoms of vitamin deficiency, which goes some way to show that supplementary doses of vitamins are rarely necessary. However, we feel from personal experience that an increased vitamin

Vitamin	Source	Symptoms of deficiency
A	Milk, butter, liver, cod liver oil, fresh green vegetables	Lowered resistance to illness; bad skin.
B	Wheat germ, yeast	Lack of appetite; indigestion; wasting.
B_2 complex (B_3, B_6, B_{12}, Choline)	Wheat germ, yeast, nuts fish, meat, milk products	Lack of appetite; indigestion; wasting.
C	Fresh green vegetables, citrus fruits	Scurvy; lowered resistance; poor healing.
D complex	Cod liver oil, eggs, cream	Poor bones (e.g. rickets).
K	Green vegetables, and body bacteria	(One form can be synthesised, so it is hardly an essential).

C intake does help to combat colds and hasten body repairs.

The accompanying table lists the more important vitamins, their sources and their uses.

Minerals are also essentials not synthesised in the body. Some minerals combine with others to carry out their function, and many of these trace elements have functions not as yet understood.

All our cells are bathed in fluid, and the correct balance of this fluid is of vital importance. The first group of minerals are necessary for this. Prolonged efforts like marathon running, particularly in high temperatures, need these minerals to maintain the proper electrolytic balance. The proper function of the electron transport chain, which is how energy gets to our muscles, depends upon the proper balance of *sodium*, *potassium* and *chlorides*.

The other group has many different functions. *Iron* combines with protein to form the oxygen-carrying haemoglobin. *Calcium* is necessary for bone growth and *magnesium* combines with calcium in this process. Minerals are essential to enzymes, the material-synthesising tools of the body, and for the correct functioning of various body processes.

An iron supplement for an athlete in heavy training is often wise. Runners seem to break up red cells more readily than non-runners, and although the body retains the iron from the haemoglobin when, after the normal lifetime (three to four months), the red blood cells break up, some extra may escape.

Women lose around 30mg of iron per month, and should certainly watch for periodic anaemia if they are considering heavy training or long-distance races, and take a supplement of iron.

Our bodies normally only take up 10 per cent of our iron intake, but will absorb more if the need is there.

Diet and Exercise – the Double Defence

Today there is a lot of talk about diseases of the heart and cardio-vascular system. Arteries become 'clogged with fatty deposits' and cholesterol is made to sound like a death sentence. It may be true that by limiting the amount of fat in the diet, and by selecting poly-unsaturated fats, this risk is reduced, but there are other factors involved. First, a genetic disposition to this kind of body disorder; and second, the amount of regular physical activity, work or exercise, that is undertaken daily.

Long-term studies on dock workers and bus crews indicated that there was a direct relationship between the absence of cardiovascular ailments and a high level of physical work and there is no doubt that a good level of physical activity, combined with a moderate, sensible diet, is the best possible preventive medicine.

But it is not just to prevent ourselves dropping dead that we want a well-controlled diet. Our main aim, more likely, is the desire to enjoy our food. On the assumption that we are starting with a good appetite – and if we are exercising efficiently we almost certainly will be – we shall not have to rely on dishes prepared solely because they are tempting. From the necessary and nourishing ingredients we need to maintain health there is plenty of tasty, enjoyable food available.

We are also likely to rely on our diet to prevent us getting fat. The genetic make-up of some people gives them a far harder battle against obesity than some of their more fortunate fellows who burn up food more quickly. But obesity is avoidable, and it is an indisputable fact that if the intake of food is regulated to the output of energy, the body will not deposit too much fat.

Since most people are to some degree overweight, the progress you make with your diet will probably be measured in terms of weight reduction. If this doesn't happen, you will simply have over-assessed the amount of food you need – i.e. you will have still been eating too much. For while we are principally concerned with running as an aid to fitness, and while we acknowledge that the overweight runner is at a disadvantage, and while we shall go on to discuss how exercise can complement a sensible diet, it must be admitted that the most powerful factor in weight control is not running or work or exercise, but food intake.

Muscle, when exercised with the appropriate loadings, will increase in strength, and with an endurance exercise such as distance running the muscles will also firm up with better muscle tone and show more definition, rather than increase in bulk. Running does not replace lost fat with muscle, it improves your muscle performance while you get trimmer. Fat is never turned into muscle, the fat cells just decrease in size.

It is a sad fact that fat is much easier to avoid than to reduce, simply because once the fat cells are laid down the number of cells remains. A reduction in fat is a reduction only of the cell size. Furthermore, the number of fat cells is fixed at adolescence, which is why it is so unkind and unfair to overfeed children.

A slim youth who puts fat on in later life is in a far better position in his attempts to reduce weight than a child who has been allowed or even encouraged to get fat and then tries to remedy his obesity when he gets older. Unnecessary weight is expensive in food and the wasted physical effort involved in carting around unwanted flesh. It places an unnecessary, even dangerous, load upon the heart. It not only requires twice the energy to lift twenty pounds as it does ten pounds, but if you try to do it at the same rate it requires a greater power output, since power is the rate at which work is done. Most fat people move more slowly because their muscular strength does not match their weight. This becomes a vicious circle because the slower they move the less exercise they take, so their muscles tend to lose strength and they end up having to move more slowly still.

All those unnecessary fat cells, wherever they are, need a blood supply, so the lungs have to supply more oxygen to the blood and the heart has to pump more blood through an enlarged vascular system and the digestive system has to convert more food to nourish useless tissue. It is as silly as that.

A Question of Balance

A balanced diet is one that allows our intake of fuel to equal, as closely as possible, the fuel we expend. Nutritionists express our energy requirements in units of heat, called calories. One calorie is the amount of heat required to raise the temperature of 1 gram of water by 1 degree centigrade. This is such a small unit that all nutrition and physiology reference is expressed in units of 1000 calories (kilocalories) expressed as Calories (or Cal.) with a capital C.

To prove that diet controls weight more effectively than exercise let's take two examples. For an untrained man in his thirties a fair performance would be running just one mile in eight minutes. If that man weighed 11 stone (70kg) he would expend energy at the rate of 15 Cal. per minute, so his mile would use up 120 Cal. But if he drinks a couple of pints of beer a day, he is adding another 2500 Cals per week. Add to that just one fish-and-chip supper while watching television one evening – 600 more Calories – and he is putting away an excess total of 3100 Cal.

To get rid of those 3100 Cal. he would have to run twenty-six miles at eight-minute mile pace. This is nearly three-and-a-half hours' hard work. It just is not on, is it? Or take the case of a forty-year-old woman who is overweight. She wants to run off a small two-ounce bar of chocolate at a slow pace. That entails running for half an hour, which is hardly worth it, and furthermore, would have to be strictly additional to her normal day's routine.

Running, to sum up, is for fitness, diet is for weight control. This does not mean however, that running is not helpful in reducing weight – it is; but dieting and running should be mutually supporting activities and are most effective when combined.

Exercising while weight-reducing has an important safety factor, in that exercise uses up the glycogen in the muscles, which increases fat utilisation. Exercise, too, prevents someone on a low calorie diet from losing lean tissue. The whole idea of dieting is to achieve that balance between input and output.

Reducing weight when you are in a poor condition is not enough. Without exercise you will only become a thin person in poor condition.

We can guess the next question: 'OK, so I need a balanced diet, but what should be in it? And, more important, how much should I eat?' There is no fixed answer to this, only what might apply to that non-existent average man or woman. A good diet should, like high level training, be geared to the individual: with proper exercise your body will change; your intake should change with it.

The first step is to get some idea of the ideal weight for you. There are several ways in which this can be done.

By taking accurate skinfold measurements at various parts of the body, the percentage of body fat in the total weight can be calculated. The figure for total weight is then adjusted to give the required body fat percentage, and this final figure is your ideal weight.

Easier, if less accurate, is to take your ideal weight from a set of tables which are compiled to consider sex and height, and sometimes age and frame as well. For distance runners, a simple estimate of desired weight is provided by the formulae of Dr Stillman who got his figures from fifty top runners in the USA. His tables are not weighted for body type or age. For men he allows 110 lb (50 kg) for a height of 5 ft, and then adds 5½ lb (2.5 kg) for each additional inch. For women the base is 100 lbs (45.5 kgs) plus 5 lb (2.27 kgs) for each additional inch. These are the average weights for non-runners; from these figures he deducts 10 per cent for ideal weights for runners.

See tables overleaf:

Height		Men Average weight			Men Ideal weight			Women Average weight			Women Ideal weight		
ft	in	st	lb	(kg)	st	lb	(kg)	st	lb	(kg)	st	lb	(kg)
5	0	7	12	(50)	7	1	(45)	7	2	(45.5)	6	6	(41)
5	1	8	3½	(52.5)	7	6	(47)	7	7	(47.7)	6	10½	(42.9)
5	2	8	9	(55)	7	11	(49.5)	7	12	(50.0)	7	1	(45)
5	3	9	0½	(57.5)	8	2	(52)	8	3	(52.3)	7	5½	(47.1)
5	4	9	6	(60)	8	7	(54)	8	8	(54.5)	7	10	(49)
5	5	9	11½	(62.5)	8	12	(56)	8	13	(56.8)	8	0½	(52.7)
5	6	10	2	(64.5)	9	3	(58.5)	9	4	(59.1)	8	5	(53.2)
5	7	10	8½	(67.5)	9	7½	(61)	9	9	(61.4)	8	9½	(55.5)
5	8	11	0	(70)	9	12½	(63)	10	0	(63.6)	9	0	(57.3)
5	9	11	5½	(72.5)	10	3½	(65)	10	5	(65.9)	9	4½	(59.3)
5	10	11	11	(75)	10	8½	(67.5)	10	10	(68.2)	9	9	(61.3)
5	11	12	2½	(77.5)	10	13½	(70)	11	1	(70.5)	9	13½	(63.5)
6	0	12	8	(80)	11	4½	(72)	11	6	(72.7)	10	4	(65.4)
6	1	12	13½	(82.5)	11	9½	(74)	11	11	(75.0)	10	8½	(67.5)
6	2	13	4	(84.5)	12	0½	(76.5)	12	2	(77.3)	10	13	(69.6)
6	3	13	9	(86.8)	12	5	(79)	12	7	(79.5)	11	3½	(71.6)

Energy intake
Recommended daily intake of protein, minerals and total calories

Age ranges	Energy	Protein recommended	Protein minimum requirement	Calcium	Iron
years	calories	g	g	mg	mg
Males					
9-11	2,500	63	36	700	13
12-14	2,800	70	46	700	14
15-17	3,000	75	50	600	15
18-34					
sedentary	2,700	68	45	500	10
moderately active	3,000	75	45	500	10
very active	3,600	90	45	500	10
35-64					
sedentary	2,600	65	43	500	10
moderately active	2,900	73	43	500	10
very active	3,600	90	43	500	10
65-74	2,350	59	39	500	10
75 and over	2,100	53	38	500	10
Females					
9-11	2,300	58	35	700	13
12-14	2,300	58	44	700	14
15-17	2,300	58	40	600	15
18-54					
most occupations	2,200	55	38	500	12
very active	2,500	63	38	500	12
55-74	2,050	51	36	500	10
75 and over	1,900	48	34	500	10
Pregnant, 2nd and 3rd trimesters	2,400	60	44	1,200	15
Lactating	2,700	68	55	1,200	15

Let us work out a simple example, to see how these tables can be used to establish a diet.

1.   You are a male, age 38 years, height 5 ft 9 in, who is moderately active in his general working day.
2.   From the Energy Intake table (page 91) we see that a moderately active man requires an intake equivalent to 2900 Cal.
3.   We will presume that you are going to run. To ensure body maintenance we will set protein at 15 per cent, fat at 20 per cent and carbohydrate at 65 per cent. This would meet the recommended requirements of a training diet.

The body converts different foods with varying degrees of efficiency, receiving roughly 4 Cal. per gram from protein, 4 Cal. per gram from carbohydrate and 9 Cal. per gram from fat.

So the first rough breakdown of your daily 2900 Cal. looks like this:

Nutrient	Percentage	Cal.	Cal. per gram	Weight of food
Protein	15	435	4	= 109 grams (3.84oz)
Fat	25	725	9	= 80 grams (2.82oz)
Carbohydrate	60	1740	4	= 435 grams (15.34oz)
Total	100	2900		624 grams (22.0oz)

A calorie intake in excess of this for this individual would mean a steady gain in weight, or a levelling off well above his ideal weight.

Now let us suppose that he is running 5 miles every alternate evening after work, an average of 17.5 miles per week. If this were run at eight-minute mile pace he would use up 15 Cal. per minute. Therefore he would get rid of an extra 2100 Cal. (17.5 x 8 x 15) per week.

$$\frac{2100 \text{ (Cal. Energy)}}{3500 \text{ (1 lb Fat)}} = 0.6 \text{ lb (9.6 oz)} = 272 \text{ g}$$

This food equivalent – rather more than half a pound of butter – is then available either to contribute to his weight loss or, if his weight is at the required level, is the amount to supplement his diet.

The calorific adjustment in this case should be on fats and carbohydrates. The fat content would not need to exceed 100 grams per day in any case, but should not be lower than the example.

Honesty Works

Be honest with yourself when you are working out the calorific value of your diet, and count the effect of nibbling and the sweet tooth. The biscuit with the tea, the additional milk or cream in tea and coffee, the sugar in those six or seven cups each day simply does not vanish. Bearing in mind that one pound of fat is the equivalent of 3500 Cal., you have only to achieve a deficit of 500 Cal. per day to lose 1 lb in a week. That doesn't sound too bad, does it? One hundred grams (just under 4 oz) of butter has a value of about 790 Cal., so a mere half-ounce saved would contribute 100 Cal. towards the reduction you seek. Likewise, an ounce less cheese would save over 100 Cal., the two-ounce chocolate bar and the two-ounce bag of peanuts each have over 250 Cals. It sounds even easier put that way, and the process can be accelerated by diminishing your food intake still further. Within limits this is quite safe, providing the meals that you eat in a day contain, after preparation, at least the minimum amounts of essential vitamins and minerals. After all, fat is stored by the body as a food reserve.

(It would be unwise to push the reduction of food intake *too* far without medical advice or the help of a good dietician, because below a certain blood-sugar level the brain will not function properly. Unless you are unwise enough to go on a severe crash diet, this is unlikely to be a danger.)

Summing up, a slimming diet should contain the essential nutrients in the correct quantities, but the total energy value must be cut. And the cuts should fall on the least essential, such as the refined sugars which are considered by some to be positively harmful. Cut down on the sugars, avoid sweets, pudding, soft drinks and alcohol. Meals that are based on lean meats, fish and eggs, with fresh fruit and vegetables, are fine. Watch the amount of bread. Cheese is good, but a little goes a long way, as it is rich in fat as well as protein. And do not go on to quack diets recommending just one or two 'specials'. You need a sensible variety of foods to avoid the risk of being deficient in essential nutrients.

Finally, once you have worked out the calorie loss required to achieve the weight reduction you want, do not forget that when you start running, if you have not already started, the extra energy you expend here must figure in your calculations. Good news for the seriously overweight person who has reduced his or her weight far enough to start running: you will now have the additional calories used up in running to help you.

Once you have achieved your ideal weight, and you still want to run, then the daily diet must cater for the increased demand. And remember, working up a good sweat is not losing weight. All you are doing is losing body fluid, which is immediately replaced from drink and food.

Meals to run on

It is one thing to write down facts and state the rules, but practicalities can modify the ideal. Most training and dieting authorities advise eating more frequently in small portions, say five small meals per day in place of three large ones. The advantages include a more even energy release, and the fact that you don't feel so hungry at any one time that each meal becomes a temptation to overeat. This is fine as long as it does not mean portions that are so small as to be uneconomic or difficult to prepare.

To give an 'ideal diet' for the runner would take a book in itself. The choice of foods is so varied that as long as each day's intake has something close to the advisable proportions of protein, fat and carbohydrate the rest is up to you.

In preparing your own menus it is useful to have a guide to the calorie content of different foods as they come from the shop. A pocket guide to branded foods is helpful, as both named products and supermarket own brands are identified with the calories by ounces and grams – we would recommend the *Pocket Calorie Guide to Branded Foods* by Alexandra Sharman.

Instead of trying to map out a whole meal-by-meal regime for the fitness runner, we will instead look at one typical meal that a runner might eat, and examine the way in which he might choose it. We will also look in some detail at a typical day's menu designed for a working woman. The latter offers a balanced choice which totals only 2248 Cal., a lot less than what we would expect an active man to need; it could therefore provide useful hints for any man seeking a fast weight loss.

Dinner for an active man who runs

Age: 32 years

Weight: 11 stone (154 lb; 70 kg)

Job: Warehouse supervisor, not office-bound. On his feet all day assisting with loading. Such an active man would need 3,600 Cal. per day, even without running.

Running: Competes a little, therefore his running is at a good pace – say 6½-minute miles. He runs 4 x 7 miles during the week, with a 10-miler on Sunday at 7-min.-mile pace. Total: about 40 miles per week. Total running time: about 4½ hours.

Running at this pace requires about 860 Cal. per hour above his 3600 Cal. 4½ x 860 Cal. = 3870 Cal. which averages 553 Cal. per day.

So his total requirement is 3600 + 553 = 4153 Cal. per day.

Since he is very active he can allow the proportion of fat in his diet to increase to 30 per cent of the calorific value, which will reduce the bulk of the meals; 15 per cent or more protein will maintain body repair and 55 per cent carbohydrate will supply the remaining energy. A sample meal is as follows:

	Weight	Cal.	Protein grams	Fat grams	Carbohydrate grams
Orange juice	(large glass)	120.0	1.2	0	28.8
Roast lamb	4oz (113g)	330.8	26.0	25.2	0
Boiled peas	3oz (85g)	32.4	4.5	0	3.6
Roast potatoes	6oz (170g)	279.6	4.8	8.4	46.2
Tinned peaches	4oz (113g)	105.6	0.4	0	26.0
Custard	3oz (85g)	103.2	3.3	3.6	14.4
Calorie conversion		971.6	40.2 × 4	37.2 × 9	119.0 × 4
Total calories in meal		971.6	160.8 (14%)	334.8 (30%)	476.0 (56%)

This meal would supply nearly a quarter of the daily food requirement. Additionally it would supply most of the daily vitamin need as follows: Calcium 43 per cent, Iron 58 per cent, Thiamin 46 per cent, Riboflavin 42 per cent, all the Nicotinic acid and Vitamin C. There is no Vitamin D, but this would be met with an ounce of average margarine from other meals.

One day with a working woman

Tea and coffee drinks, of course, are mainly composed of water, but the amount of tea or coffee varies considerably. These arbitary figures have been used in the menu below: tea ⅙ oz, coffee ⅒ oz.

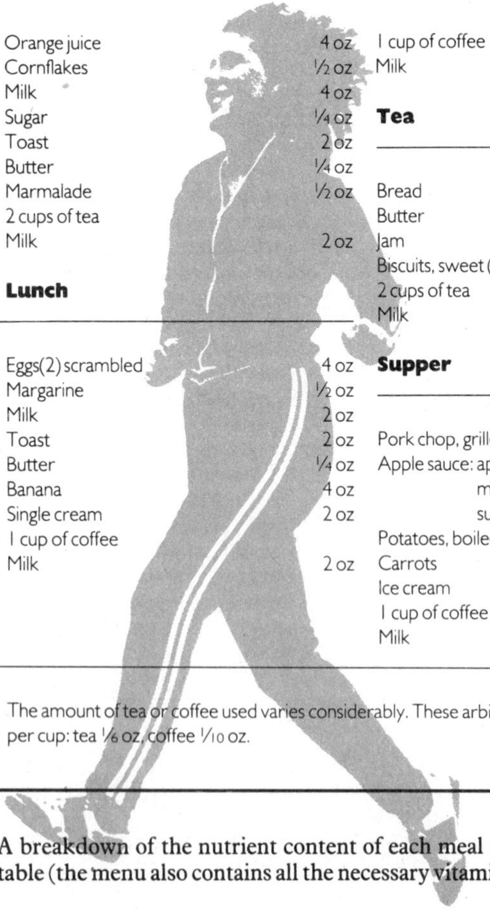

one day with a working woman

Breakfast

Orange juice	4 oz
Cornflakes	½ oz
Milk	4 oz
Sugar	¼ oz
Toast	2 oz
Butter	¼ oz
Marmalade	½ oz
2 cups of tea	
Milk	2 oz

Lunch

Eggs (2) scrambled	4 oz
Margarine	½ oz
Milk	2 oz
Toast	2 oz
Butter	¼ oz
Banana	4 oz
Single cream	2 oz
I cup of coffee	
Milk	2 oz

Snack

I cup of coffee	
Milk	2 oz

Tea

Bread	I oz
Butter	⅛ oz
Jam	½ oz
Biscuits, sweet (2)	½ oz
2 cups of tea	
Milk	2 oz

Supper

Pork chop, grilled	4 oz
Apple sauce: apple	4 oz
margarine	⅕ oz
sugar	¼ oz
Potatoes, boiled	6 oz
Carrots	4 oz
Ice cream	2 oz
I cup of coffee	
Milk	2 oz

The amount of tea or coffee used varies considerably. These arbitrary figures have been used per cup: tea ⅙ oz, coffee ⅒ oz.

A breakdown of the nutrient content of each meal is shown in the following table (the menu also contains all the necessary vitamins and minerals).

Meal	Cal.	Protein grams	Fat grams	Carbo— hydrate grams
Breakfast	462	11.4	13.6	75.0
Snack	39	2.2	2.2	2.9
Lunch	729	25.0	46.1	57.5
Tea	232	5.0	8.9	35.3
Supper	786	40.2	38.6	76.6
Total dietary intake	2,248	83.8	109.4	247.3

The Snack Trap
One more quick example, just to convince those people who say that they don't eat much – only snacks:

One snack lunch: white bread, butter, cheese, lettuce, tomato, instant coffee, milk. Total weight – slightly over 10 oz (282 g). Total Calories – 643.3

One cooked lunch: Roast lamb, fried potatoes (chips), boiled peas, tinned peaches, custard. Total weight – 14½ oz (410 g). Total Calories – 646.5

The snack is giving the body almost exactly the same number of calories as the cooked meal – and any self-congratulation by the snack-eater on his abstinence is demonstrably misplaced.

Diet deficiences do not manifest themselves at once. If in any one week your intake is short of iron or vitamin C or whatever, you will not break out in spots during the following week.

While we lack an early warning system for dietary deficiencies there is also plenty of time in the following week to make up for the one week's shortfall. What we are saying is that an obsessional concern with milligrams per day of anything is neither necessary nor advisable.

Most people think of malnutrition as meaning not enough but this is only partly true. Malnutrition means bad nutrition, and too much is also bad.

Some athletes have trouble keeping their weight down even when they are in full training. Others, like Seb, have a much easier time:

'I'm lucky, really, I just don't seem to be *able* to eat too much. As long as I'm sensible I just never seem to put on weight.

This is a tremendous advantage. I do try to make sure that I get the benefit of the proper ingredients for my diet – potatoes in their jackets rather than potatoes boiled away to nothing, for example, and enough salads and enough meat – but after that I can literally eat just what I want. I've never been overweight, as far as I can remember. In fact if I ever did have a problem it would probably be to maintain weight rather than lose it.

Oddly enough I find that during the track season, when I'm training hardest. I probably eat slightly *less* than when I'm doing easier work in the winter months. It's probably just that like everyone else I'm eating more in the winter to maintain body heat; and I must say that in the summer, after a long, hard track session, I physically don't *want* to eat for two or three hours.

All this makes it fairly easy for me. I usually have a cooked breakfast, a reasonably light salad lunch, and a proper cooked dinner in the evening. The evening meal is often quite late – I sometimes don't finish my training till well into the early evening, and I certainly can't eat straight after that, I do tend to nibble a bit between meals, too. I've got a sweet tooth, and I'm a sucker for chocolate biscuits.

I'm a bit more particular about drinking. I just cannot run with drink inside me – I tend to get the most awful stomach cramps.

When I run first thing in the morning I may have just a quarter of a cup of tea to help the body start working, but really I'd prefer to run with nothing inside me at all. Before a race I wouldn't dream of drinking within four or four-and-a-half hours of the start. That's going to be a problem if I ever run a marathon; you really do have to drink in a race as long as that, but the idea of running with a lot of liquid swilling about inside doesn't bear thinking about.

Otherwise, though, I drink quite a lot. Not straight after a run – I don't seem to need it then – but during the rest of the day I can get through plenty of cups of tea or coffee, as well as a pint of milk at lunchtime and perhaps a pint or so of fruit juice during the course of the evening.

The one time that I might make diet concessions of any sort is when I'm racing abroad, particularly in the warmer climates. I'm careful not to eat ice-cream or fresh salads, say, or unpeeled fruit or sea food; and I stick to bottled water to drink. Some athletes have a terrible time abroad, they never seem to step off a plane without getting stomach trouble; Brendan Foster used to be a perennial victim, and poor David Moorcroft was on a strict diet of bread and jam from the moment he arrived in Athens for the European Championships last year. I've never been as unlucky as that, and I'd probably be all right whatever I ate. But it would be stupid to ruin a race just by being careless about food.'

The Alcohol Question

If it came to a straightforward case of do or don't the answer would have to be don't. Unfortunately life isn't all that simple; a lot of people enjoy a drink, and we have to make value judgments. It is the potential of alcohol that is the biggest problem. The potential for good is just about non-existent and the potential for harm is infinite.

Alcohol is a depressant and gives the illusion of relaxing the drinker. In fact it anaesthetises the nerves but not, unless drunk to excess, the muscles. What passes for acceptable social imbibing is not enough to relax muscles, and it certainly cannot remove stress symptoms.

So what does it do? Most relevant to the runner is the fact that alcohol constricts the arteries leading to the heart, it has an adverse effect at submaximal work loads by decreasing oxygen uptake, it upsets the delicate heat balance mechanism of the body, it impairs co-ordination, and it generally deludes the drinker into believing that things are better than they are. Alcohol can also destroy some essential nutrients, like the vitamin B group. Excess alcohol can also cause hypoglycaemia, and the brain cannot function properly with a low blood sugar level. And alcohol is not good for the liver, which is our glycogen storehouse.

The only pressure to take alcohol is a social one, and a romanticised one at that. It is regrettable that many of our so-called hearty sportsmen – and rugger players, for example, figure prominently among them – are obviously over-weight and not very fit. Furthermore alcohol is fattening: 1 pint of beer equals 250 Cal.

But old habits die hard, and some acquired tastes will not go away. The answer must be a compromise – less than perfect, but tolerable.

For example, Seb's compromise works like this: 'From the end of February to the end of September I drink very little alcohol. When I do, it is no more than a sipped toast at the odd reception or, equally rarely, a small glass of lemonade shandy. The replacement I use is a double Britvic orange juice with enough lemonade to fill a pint glass. For me winter drinking is an occasional half of Guinness or a lemonade shandy if I'm thirsty. I do enjoy a single glass of wine at dinner sometimes, but once serious training has commenced – no more alcohol.'

To say there are no drinking distance runners would be ridiculous, and tolerance varies with individuals, but it is our observation that intake varies inversely with your belief in your own potential. The better you believe you can be, the less you'll drink. Funnily enough, drink can be used as a good excuse for failing. 'Ah yes, I could be a lot better but I like my beer,' is a frequently heard cop-out. But if fun runners and fitness runners can still measure improvement on an occasional beer or glass of wine, then what they are drinking is all right for them.

Taking Up the Challenge

Now that you have some solid running behind you, the chances are that you will be looking ahead with fresh eyes – perhaps with ambitions that a few weeks ago you wouldn't have thought possible, perhaps with your sights now firmly on a target you set yourself years ago. Not everyone will be looking ahead to an Olympic final, but every runner will at some time or another be tempted to test his or her improved abilities on a set course or over a classic distance against the clock – and in contention with, or at least in the company of, runners of similar ability. It would be very strange if, one day, you didn't respond to the temptation.

Whenever the talk gets round to running, one question is asked more than any other: 'How much running should be done?'

Whether the aim is to run for fitness or to run for an Olympic gold medal, the reply is still the same: just enough and no more than is necessary to achieve your goal; anything more is likely to be counter-productive.

If you are aiming to be the best, then the training load will be high, but as soon as your performance levels off then you have done enough. You can examine your training schedules to see if there should be a shift of emphasis, but do not simply do more – it takes less training to maintain your condition than it does to achieve it, and while it takes 80 per cent of your maximum to apply a stimulus strong enough to bring about an improvement, it takes only a 60 per cent loading to maintain that level.

The principle is equally true with running for fitness. Once you have achieved the level you want, cut back a little and do only enough to stay fit. If you decide to compete, then you change your routine to sharpen up, but only enough to reach your new target.

And fun running is the simplest of all. First you get fit enough to run freely without strain, and then you run for fun. If you want more fun, then you run some more, and this becomes its own training. But as soon as the amount of running becomes a chore, or you start suffering undue aches and pains, you will just naturally reduce the load.

There is a general rule which says you should finish your runs feeling well worked but mentally fresh, and certainly not physically exhausted. For nearly all situations outside racing this is very true, but for the ambitious there are times when exceptions have to be made in training.

The following conversation will illustrate the point:

Peter: 'He's a nice looking runner, he has the right build and style and strength. He really should be a lot better than he is.'

Seb: 'Yes I know, Dad, but he's turned eighteen and he hasn't yet learned how to hurt himself. And I don't think he ever will.'

What Seb was saying was cruel but true: all of us can keep going that bit longer than we think, if only we are prepared to find out. Part of the art of coaching is to have a nose for the right level of development, and the right moment for your charge to test himself in this way. Runners with ambition will have to go through this more than once and not leave it only to race days.

This brings in another factor in determining what is enough. Enough is what the whole man, not just the body, will accept. The work load may be within the limit set by your body but if you mentally reject that amount of training, then it becomes too much. The sad fact is that if you cannot mentally accept what you are doing, your body will ultimately reject it as well, and you will not extract from the exercise the physical benefits you should.

Keeping the Record Straight

A training diary is well worth while. If you hate writing even a single line it may be a tedious job, but it's going to be a lot easier than the training stints you're going to be setting yourself, and the end product will be both interesting and valuable.

It doesn't have to be anything elaborate – an ordinary scribbling diary or exercise book will do. And all you have to record is the day, the mileage you run, your time for the distance, the weather, the state of your health that day, and your feelings or impressions during and after the run.

What is the point? For some of you it may be no more than a personal journal, which will be pleasant to look through and reminisce over in the years to come; but it could be much more useful than that. It will help you to check your overall adherence to your training plan. It will allow you to identify actions or events which prove to suit your training – or not to suit it. It may enable you to relate any improvement, or any injury, to some specific facet of your training. And in time it will indicate expected recovery time from any setback you may suffer – colds, flu, minor injuries and the effects of any lay-off period.

We still refer to one or more of the 'historic' build-ups when we are planning for a big event. There is no reason why you, in your own way, shouldn't benefit in the same way.

A Choice of Targets

Everyone will have their own targets, and there is no point in trying to give detailed training schedules to them all. So we are going to look at a number of runners with widely varying ambitions, and chart their progress towards those goals. We will guide our novice fitness runner towards a local fun-run type of race; our more confident fitness runner to a season of modest road racing or cross-country; our established fitness runner, who we assume will have been running steadily for a few years, towards a first-time marathon – and we'll see how an accomplished athlete prepares for a top-class international middle-distance championship. None of these may fit your own requirements precisely, but one of them, we are sure, will adapt readily to what you are looking for.

The Three-mile Fun Run

The local community centre has a member who is a regular club runner, and they have persuaded him to put on a short road race as part of their Fitness Week.

You have already been running for fitness and pleasure and feel a little glow of satisfaction at your progress and now, quite suddenly, you want to know. You want to know if you are as good as you think you are and as good as you feel. You have posted your entry form and now you find that you have barely a month to go to the race. 'What should I be doing now?' you ask. That's the easy bit – but . . .

You know that your nine-year-old son will settle for nothing less than a Dave Moorcroft runaway victory and, worse still, he hates the kid next door, whose healthy dad jumps the front garden gate every morning. And of course his dad has also entered – a happy piece of news your own lad couldn't wait to tell you.

So now the question 'What should I be doing?' (like emigrating?) takes on a new urgency.

Now, how long have you got? A month? Oh well, hard luck, you should have bought our book two months ago. Never mind, we will see what we can do. Three things before you start:

Rule 1: Play it cool – don't even tell your son what you're at. Act nonchalantly and don't let the enemy know what you are doing.

Rule 2: Don't panic – think.

Rule 3: Start from the bottom up – let's look at your feet.

Question: Are the shoes you are running in now going to be all right in four weeks' time? Never turn out in a new pair of shoes, that's a real trouble risk. The modern shoes with nylon tops and waffle soles are easy to get used to, but get them now: that way they will be OK to race in after a month. If you are going to need a repair before race day, get it done *now*. And have put aside a *tried* pair of clean socks.

Examine your feet carefully for any actual or potential trouble spots, like toenails that are growing in at the corners, corns on top or between your toes, blisters or hot spots. Once you have checked over your feet, try to keep them in condition all the time.

You are going to *race* over a three-mile course, not merely run it. What is comfortable when you are proceeding at your own pace quickly becomes exhausting if it's done too quickly, so start concentrating on pace judgment now.

Even for a beginner certain basic rules apply. If you are going to race 3 miles, train for at least 4. You will need the strength and confidence of knowing that you can last 4 hard miles. Now break down the required 3-mile time into minutes per mile. For example if your goal is 3 miles in 19½ minutes then your pace is at 6½ minutes per mile.

From here on your training splits three ways. The first will be steady over-distance running for good all-round stamina, say a run of 6–8 miles.

The second way is running a mile at race pace or better, having a short recovery, say 2–3 minutes, and then continuing for another mile with another short recovery of 2–3 minutes and then complete the third mile. Each mile should be run at least race pace.

The third line of attack will be to run 1 mile at race pace and continue at the same pace until you start to slow significantly. You will extend this type of running until you are able to run for 4 miles at your 3-mile race pace. Your month's schedule can now be planned. (A note about planning: if you have a regular hobby evening or a family activity like swimming every Tuesday evening, or your wife has a regular evening class and you are looking after the home, make that day your rest day. Then plan the days round that rest day. This avoids family disruption and guilt feelings on all sides).

Just to start somewhere we will assume that Wednesday is to be your rest day, and the race is planned for the Sunday four weeks from now.

Week 1

Monday
Run 6 miles steady at your comfortable pace
Tuesday
1 mile in 6½ mins. Jog home (J.H.) if you are training within a mile or two of your home
Wednesday
Rest
Thursday
1 mile in 6½ min. Rest 3 min. Run 1 mile in 6½ min
Friday
6 miles steady (as Monday)
Saturday
1½ miles in 9¾ min (J.H.)
Sunday
6 miles steady

Week 2

Monday
3 × 1 mile at 6½-min pace, with a 3-min rest between each mile (J.H.)
Tuesday
6 miles steady
Wednesday
Rest
Thursday
2 miles in 13 min (J.H.)
Friday
6 miles steady
Saturday
4 × 1 mile at 6½-min pace, with a 2-min rest between each mile (J.H.)
Sunday
6 miles steady

Week 3

Monday
2½ miles in 16¼ min (J.H.)
Tuesday
6 miles steady
Wednesday
Rest
Thursday
4 × 1 mile at 6½-min pace, with 1½-min rest between each mile (J.H.)
Friday
8 miles steady
Saturday
3 miles in 19½ min (J.H.)
Sunday
6 miles steady

Week 4

Monday
3½ miles in 22¾ min (J.H.)
Tuesday
8 miles steady
Wednesday
Rest
Thursday
4 × 1 mile at 6½-min pace, with ½-min rest between each mile (J.H.)
Friday
3 miles easy
Saturday
Rest
Sunday
RACE

(On the rest days and whenever you can – each day if possible – do plenty of bending and stretching to avoid feelings of stiffness.)

There, that wasn't so bad, was it?

Now that you have successfully completed your first competitive run you will have the desire and confidence to continue racing.

You will also have had enough running to start using, cautiously, the interval training we described in Chapter Four. This should improve your oxygen uptake and yield an improvement in your road running endurance and speed.

To begin with we would suggest sessions of 10 (working up to 20) x 100 metres in 18 sec, with 40 sec walk or jog recovery. Start doing this twice a week and then, after a month, increase the distance to 10 (working up to 20) x 200 metres in 38–40 sec with 60 sec recovery.

A Season on the Road

After a bit more training, and a few successful races to test your confidence and prove that you are, indeed, getting stronger, you may decide that you would like to try road racing in a limited way.

This time, though, you have made your decision well in advance – full of the joys of fitness running and celebrating Christmas, you decide to enter a number of road events later in the coming year.

Because you will be able to spend months rather than weeks on your build-up you will be in a position to introduce some more specialised and specific elements into your training. Sessions of interval training, speed endurance and fartlek will all have their place.

The events you will probably be considering are the increasingly popular 10 kilometre (6¼ mile) road races. If you are under thirty a first-time target of 40 minutes on a slightly undulating course is realistic. For the trim and fit forty-year-old the expectation is somewhat lower; a time around 46–48 minutes is a fair performance.

The following schedules, starting in January, should produce the right results six or seven months later. The four weeks after Christmas are taken up with carefully consolidating the new weekly mileage, and from then on you will train on a schedule of overall increasing mileage. The weeks that contain one or two of the fartlek, interval or speed endurance sessions will contain a lower mileage, both because they can be quite hard training sessions, and because they take up more time for fewer miles. Also, in terms of mileage it is helpful to run alternate hard and easy weeks.

This schedule should not be too hard for a runner under thirty. The 48-minute forty-year-old may feel he has to add a half a minute per mile to his earlier training pace, but he should try, without straining, to get closer to the under-thirties schedule towards the end.

The mileage chart is drawn to cover seven periods, each of four weeks, and each week should contain one rest day. This day is not an active rest day (if it's a Sunday, for example, it is not for long walks, cycle rides or a lot of swimming), it is for relaxation. It's not an absolutely fixed day but it should be well spaced at as close to weekly intervals as possible.

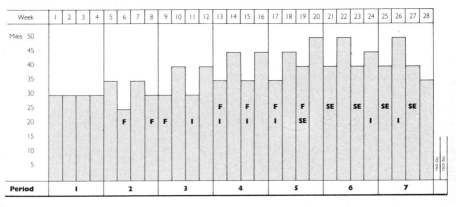

Week	1	2	3	4	5	6	7	8	9	10	11	12	13	14	15	16	17	18	19	20	21	22	23	24	25	26	27	28
													F	F		F	F	SE	SE		SE	SE						
					F		F	F		I		I	I		I	SE			I		I							
Period	1		2			3			4			5			6			7										

F indicates Fartlek session   **I** indicates Interval session   **SE** indicates Speed Endurance session

(Always warm up properly before these three sessions – say 2 miles – and 'jog down' 1 mile afterwards.)

For your *interval training*, take your best time for 200 metres and increase this by 20 per cent (e.g. best 200 metres is 28 sec, interval training pace is 28 + 5.6 sec = 33.6, say 34–35 sec per 200 metres). The recovery period between runs should be about three times the duration of the run (about 1½ min) and should be walked or jogged.

Your *speed endurance* runs should be around 800 metres to 1000 metres. Cyclometers and the trips on car speedos usually read off in tenths of a mile, so if you are using one of these to check a distance, then settle for the five tenths and six tenths marks on the clock. These are 880 yards and 1056 yards respectively. The pace for these runs should be based upon your best time for the distance plus 25 per cent. (This pace is one suggested only for a runner at this stage of improvement; it is not correct for faster track athletes.) The recovery should be twice the running time (e.g. best half mile time of 2 min 25 sec + 36.25 sec = 3 min 1.25 sec – say 3 min). Therefore run for 3 minutes and walk/jog recovery for 6 minutes.

Period I

Weeks 1-4
6 daily runs each of 5 miles steady running,
7min 30sec per mile pace for 4 weeks

Period II

Week 5
as above but daily average of 6 miles
Week 6
5 days of 4 miles at 7min per mile pace; 1 day
of 5 miles of fartlek
Week 7
as week 5
Week 8
5 days of 4-5 miles; 1 hour of fartlek

Period III

Week 9
as week 8
Week 10
6 days of 6-7 miles at 7min to 7min 30sec per
mile pace
Week 11
5 days of 5 miles at 7min per mile pace
Week 12
as week 10

Period IV

Week 13
4 days of 7 miles (7min pace); 1-day intervals;
1 day fartlek (1 hour)
Week 14
5 days of 5 miles (7min pace); 1 day of 10 miles
(7min 30sec pace)
Week 15
as week 13
Week 16
as week 14

Period V

Week 17
as week 13
Week 18
as week 14
Week 19
4 days of 7 miles (7min 30sec pace); 1 day
fartlek (1 hour); 1 day speed endurance (4 ×
800m)
Week 20
5 days (6,8,6,8,7 miles at 7-7min 30sec pace);
1 day 10 miles at (7min 30sec pace)

Period VI

Week 21
5 days of 7 miles (7min pace); 1 day speed
endurance (5 × 800m)
Week 22
4 days of 8 miles (7min pace); 1 day 12 miles
(7min 30sec pace)
Week 23
as week 21
Week 24
5 days of 8 miles (7min pace); 1 day intervals

Period VII

Week 25
as week 21
Week 26
as week 22
Week 27
as week 21
Week 28
5 days (9,8,7,6,5 miles) 9,8,7 miles at 7min -7min
30sec pace; 6 & 5 miles at 6min 30sec-7min
pace

Take a complete rest the day before a race. If you are under thirty, depending upon your general condition, you might very well crack the target times, but at the end of this schedule running 40 to 45 miles per week will allow you to race over distances of 3 to 6 miles every three weeks from August to October inclusive. Don't forget to do plenty of suppleness exercises.

Do not mix the fartlek or interval sessions with the steady runs, keep them for separate days – a steady run on one day, fartlek or intervals on another.

A Winter in the Mud

Training for a cross-country season will not be as specific as that for a series of road races, but the following suggestions will help any runner with a background of stamina and fitness running who wants to have a go over the country.

You will need plenty of mixed road work, fast runs over 4–6 miles for sustained pace, and plenty of steady runs over 10 miles or more for stamina. Repetition speed endurance sessions with runs over 800, 1000 and 1200 metres should also be included in your training.

If you cannot find a circuit in a hilly park or a bit of open country of, say, 2-mile laps, then you will have to find the features you want separately and practise on them in turn. Training on hills in town can be hard and useful but never quite the same – your footing is much firmer and safer in town, and the hard surfaces won't develop the ankle strength that lets you run over rough ground without worry.

Learning how to pick the best parts of a course where it is easier or safer to overtake other runners comes only with experience. Learn to gauge when the little bit of path or road can be safely negotiated with spikes, or to know at a glance when you are going to need the 15mm spikes for a grip, or whether ripples or waffles are going to be the better bet. If you do wear spikes, a heel wedge will be kinder on your calves and achilles tendons.

It is easier to perform reasonably over 10km on the road than it is at this distance over the country, particularly if you are training on a restricted mileage. The very best cross-country runner would need an average of 60–65 good miles per week at least to race well over the country, although it is doubtful if a 9-mile 'National' could be won even on this mileage.

The Lure of the Marathon

Welcome to another 'I want to know' case – the man who wants to say 'I have run the marathon'. It could very well be someone just like you.

You have seen the mass marathons on television and you know that just finishing is, for you, not enough. There are times returned in these events which preclude the possibility that the finishers actually ran the whole distance. They might have walked, crawled or swum it, but they never ran it. Out of respect for the sport and for yourself, and bearing in mind your age and the demands of your job, you have come up with a time of four hours as your target.

This is the best time that you can realistically expect. The decision to attempt the marathon is not one that is taken lightly, and you have delayed the moment of final commitment until you have only four months left before the race. Luckily for you this makes it an end-of-season event, when the autumn weather should be ideal.

Your background is fairly typical. You took up jogging a couple of years ago rather sporadically, but all last year you made a serious effort to train, and in fact got up to an average of 30 miles a week. You have a decent job where you are paid for your knowledge and ability rather than your time, and your colleagues are sympathetic to your endeavour – in fact you have got them to sponsor you per mile for charity. For someone who is not an established athlete and is strictly a fitness and fun runner, your background is ideal for success, particularly as you are not coming home whacked from contract bricklaying or concreting. What you have to do is to get in enough distance running before the day, check your diet, and pay attention to those particular aspects of running that are problems only in marathons.

Let's take mileage first. Our good friend Trevor Wright, a Sheffield athlete of great talent and experience, says that he thinks that 70–75 miles a week is quite enough mileage to run a good marathon. This may seem low to some runners aiming for the top. We will always agree that training schedules should be individually prescribed but Trevor won a silver medal in the European Championship in his first marathon in 1971 and recently ran a 2 hour 12 minute marathon. His record in cross-country and at 10,000 metres on the track is also a fine one, and he won the King of the Road title a few years back.

Now although much can be done by those at the top on 75 miles a week, it is still a lot of miles to be found, and for runners not as fast as Trevor Wright, even more time is required for the same mileage.

Furthermore, to go mad suddenly on increasing mileage at this stage is inviting the athlete to break down. The total mileage wants lifting, but very carefully and steadily – and we do not propose to set our first-time man more than 50 miles in any one week.

What prospective marathon runners must do is to establish their pace judgment. Your aim is to achieve a time of four hours for the race. If you get the feel of this pace firmly established it will help you to assess by the mid-stages of the race if you are going to be able to sustain it over the latter part of the race. If not, then you must choose one of only two options open to you. First, to see how far you can go at that pace, a good piece of knowledge in itself, or second, note the mile mark at which you are still on target, and then deliberately slow down in order to complete the distance.

This decision should be made with the following in mind. Is it a 'one-off' event to satisfy the desire to say 'I ran a marathon' or is it to say 'I set out for a four hour marathon and if it eludes me this time, next time I will succeed.'? If it is the latter then you must take the first choice and stick to your pace.

We cannot advise on this choice except to say that we based Seb's athletic career on the premise that once the target is identified you go for broke. For a marathon runner, it is best taken before the race, as it significantly changes the runner's attitude – and hence his performance – on the day.

Now, back to the problem of pace and mileage in training. Four months – or about seventeen weeks – is the time beween now and the race.

The general plan is this: learn pace judgment on the shorter runs and steadily extend the longer runs to approach the racing distance. Later on some of the shorter runs will be faster than race pace and some, or part of some, of the longer runs will be at race pace.

A marathon is 26 miles 385 yards, and to run it in four hours means a pace of 9 min 9 sec per mile. In order to get your pace judgment accurate measure off parts of your training roads – five mile sections are long enough – and during your training runs make sure that you run enough of these sections between 45 min 30 sec and 46 min in order to get the feel of the pace.

Throughout your four-month build-up there will be – and there should be – a

Marathon training chart

Week	Tues	Weds	Thurs	Fri	Sat	Sun	Mon	Total
1	6	5	ss	6	5	8	ss	30
2	5	6	ss	5	6	10	ss	32
3	6	6	ss	6	6	10	ss	34
4	6	8	ss	8	6	8	ss	36
5	5	8	ss	8	5	12	ss	38
6	10	6	ss	9	7	8	ss	40
7	11	5	ss	9	7	9	ss	41
8	6	7	ss	7	6	16	ss	42
9	6	8	6	8	6	10	ss	44
10	10	7	ss	10	7	12	ss	46
11	6	8	ss	8	6	20	ss	48
12	6	10	8	10	8	8	ss	50
13	12	5	6	6	5	16	ss	50
14	6	10	6	10	6	10	ss	48
15	7	10	ss	7	ss	16	ss	40
16	5	6	ss	6	8	8	ss	33
17	6	jog 5	jog 4	ss	ss	RACE		15

Training total 667

(ss = suppleness and stretching on rest day)

lot of mileage that you will run at faster than race pace and this running will be all to your good, but do remember to refresh your memory from time to time as to what 9 min 9 sec pace is really like. This judgment will be essential on the race day, because assuming you get through this schedule, eat properly and sleep well, the first ten miles of your marathon are going to feel easy; the real danger will be getting carried away with how well you are going and trying to cover too many miles and get too many minutes to the good; this will lead to a desperately hard last five miles.

Also, on the eleventh week of the schedule, there is a twenty-mile run. Do not, even if you still feel very good, get the wild idea of finishing the full marathon distance just to know you can do it a month later. Remember, you are training for your first marathon, not for two in one month.

You will notice that, with exception of weeks 9, 12, 13 and 14, the pattern of days 'off' and 'on' is one off, two on, one off, three on. In the event of enforced lay-offs (colds, for example) return to the exact pattern as soon as possible. If you are not feeling fully fit, return to the daily pattern at a reduced pace and/or mileage, but keep to the pattern.

All over the country runners make their long runs on a Sunday. Club runners particularly use this day and we feel that for those runners who enjoy their running more when in company this will always be the day. There may be work or domestic reasons that rule out Saturday anyway, but if after a hard Sunday run you do not feel fresh enough to face work on Monday, consider moving the mileage build-up chart back one day. This would give you an old-fashioned lay-about Sunday and ensure a better Monday.

Being fresh for work is important because any carry-over of business or domestic worries into an otherwise smooth-running preparation will have an adverse effect on the training and ultimately the race. However, the great majority of runners are 'long run Sunday' people, and you should cope with this quite happily. If you do want an easy Sunday, try not to swop in and out of Saturday and Sunday as you go along. The mileage chart is drawn up to give you adequate recovery during each and every week and the last four days before your race are to give you a chance to feed up, rest and store the glycogen.

During this seventeen-week period the diet must be watched, because in some weeks there is going to be a big increase in the total mileage.

The less useless weight a runner carries around with him the better, particularly a marathon runner, and the first eight weeks of our schedule might well be used to get rid of the few excess pounds you may be carrying.

In our chapter on diet and nutrition, we noted that a man in a sedentary job needs around 2600 Cal. per day. Running at about 7 mph requires about 870 Cal. per hour, so a forty-mile-week will need an additional 5000 Cal. per week, or 714 Cal. per day. Nevertheless, by week 11 weight changes should be stabilised and from then on a careful check should be maintained on weight control.

If the extra running does increase your hunger, eat more frequently – not more. Certainly if your percentage of body fat was correct before you started on this schedule, you should be matching the increase in mileage with a balanced addition to your diet, somewhere between 100 and 125 Cal. per mile per week.

As far as your mile-chart is concerned, remember that a top athlete going for a big marathon would have a significantly different build-up for his attempt than the one suggested for you. To start with, his programme would be spread over the year, and although he might race more than one marathon, he would always keep the big one in mind and his training would always be biased towards this race.

Furthermore, his total mileage would be at least double yours, and would very likely alternate the hard months with easy ones. While there would be an overall climb in mileage as the training progressed, there would probably be a 'macro-recovery period' every other month. In other words, a hard month is followed by a full month of lower mileage to fully recover and consolidate the improvement laid down by the stress of the hard month. Inside this overall plan would still be a 'micro-recovery period' such as one day hard and one or two days easy.

But your case is a rush job of four months – and you are not an athlete conditioned to a sixty-miles-per-week base from which to start.

The plan you have provides for a small, steady increase week by week until you reach fifty miles per week which is then held for two weeks. Though people have completed, and doubtless will complete, marathons on lower mileages, we would consider this to be about the lowest total weekly distance on which some one relatively inexperienced might expect to manage four hours in reasonable comfort.

What relief from over-stressing that can be allowed inside the time scale must be achieved during the week. The longest runs are nearly all followed by a rest day; if not, they follow one.

A Tilt at the Championship

For our final example we will suppose a big track championship meeting somewhere in Europe in August or September when three races – heat, semi-final and final – will be required.

We will also suppose our athlete is someone like Seb. For this kind of athlete there is no particular build-up in his training, you cannot bring world class athletes to the 'boil' quickly, certainly not with any likelihood of consistency. For a main event of this importance the whole year's training will be organised towards this goal, although he will have run some good-class one-offs before this. It may take five or six fast races to consolidate his speed and form before he sets out to win a major event.

We can only give an outline of a training year, and then detail the last two weeks before the big event.

The athlete will have built up a solid strength and endurance base by steady distance running and by hard weight and circuit training in the gymnasium. On to this base, using a multi-tier training programme as in our sample schedule, he will build up speed endurance – the ability, in this case, to run one half-mile flat out and then one mile nearly flat out. In addition, he will not have neglected his pure sprinting speed.

For this kind of performer the last two weeks before the race is not a build-up period, this has been done already; no, this period is better considered as a count-down time.

It would require a different kind of book to chart the fine deails of 'periodising' and specific build-up for world-class runners, but the following is a generalised scheme.

September: end of season.

October: ideally a holiday by the sea, somewhere mild and warm.

November to February: train 13 days out of 14 with runs of 6–12 miles (10–20 km) plus weight training and circuit training.

March to May: start this period as above, but introduce more hill work (hard repetition running up slopes of 100–1000 metres long), while increasing the speed content of the training. This is the main period of multi-tier training. Starting around 40 miles per week in November and working up to 65–80 miles per week by March, the mileage will then decrease as the speed content of training increases.

The main distance work will be done on road and grass as steady running. Then will come some interval training, followed by sustained speed over relatively short distances – say 600–1000 metres.

Into this training will be worked sessions of sharp sprinting speed and speed sessions such as 6 x 300 metres flat out with short recoveries and 8 x 400 metres at 95 per cent effort.

June to September: this is the main racing season, and throughout this period he will have to maintain general condition and speed with only one or two easy days before any race. Weight training and circuit training are finished by the middle or end of May.

October: brings the year full circle, with the prospect of a non-working holiday where only walking and swimming interrupts relaxation. The mental refreshment is even more important than the physical relief from the hard training.

That is a very broad summary of the way a top middle-distance runner might organise his year. Peter Coe gives a more detailed insight into the rigorous schedule he and Sebastian might devise for an important season:

'**November, December, January**: *5000m work.*
One short run – (9–14 km) on 5 days per week;
One long run – (16–19 km) on 1 day per week.
Additionally there will be on 2–3 days per week sessions that will be repetition running. These runs will be over distances from 100m to 1000m, all with short recoveries – usually jogging. When the total distances are low, weight training will be held twice per week, plus a circuit training session of 1 hour 30min. If the mileage is high or there are additional repetition sessions, then the circuit training may have to be omitted and only one weight session taken. One important note: always finish a session of running on an 'up-temp' note, i.e. in 95–100 per cent effort over the last 300–400 metres of a distance run.

Hill running for power. Having said that the kind of speed we want has to be sustained speed, we apply this principle to hill running when using 100m and 200m distances. These short distances are semi-sprint sessions which build up to 30–40 repetitions over the 100m and up to 10 repetitions for the 200m.

The 100m slope is approximately 10 degrees, and the recovery is an immediate jog back down the hill. The 200m slope is about 7 or 8 degrees with a jog back recovery: this run is performed at about 90 per cent effort.

The long hill work is on a 1000m incline, on one single set of 6 runs with a slow run back. Our hill is largely anaerobic and develops the ability to maintain good form when working hard. A high knee lift and a vigorous arm action has to be maintained throughout these runs.

Around April, the first time in England when the weather is suitable in our part of the country, we use a particular kind of hill running which is a coach-controlled type of fartlek training (except that there is not much play in it). It is fast and slow running around a grassy hill during which the athlete must sprint flat out between signals. The coach signals the start and finish of the sprint with a blast on a whistle. This way the runner has to respond to another's command (a track situation) and not when he feels like it. The coach chooses the flat section or the up or down part of the circuit; he varies the sprinting time from 7–15 sec and the continuous jogging recovering depending upon how long he wants the session to last. This varies between 12 and 25 minutes. This is very demanding, and is not for every runner as there is the danger of a severe 'breaking down' effect.

General distance work: Most distance running will be run at 3min 20sec per kilometre pace, although occasionally during a 15 or 16km run the last 8km will be run at 3min per km pace as a check on general condition.

February, March, April, May: Multi-tier training (see schedule) plus one long run of 16–19km per week. Weight training and circuit training is still continued, but now some track sessions are shared with a 400m squad. Plus the following:

March: Careful build up towards sprinting speed using 60m to 80m work and shuttle runs in a gymnasium.

April: Flat out repetitions with 400m squad over 150m, 200m, and 300m (conditions permitting – keeping warm at all times).

May: When the pure sprinters take longer intervals, the 800/1500 man puts in extra repetitions; this is also the time to commence hard speed endurance sessions over 600m and 800m.

May, June: Serious weight training is finished by mid-May and only general light sessions of medium repetitions on a multi-gym machine are used about once a week and the remainder of the work will be either pure sprinting, 60m–80m accelerations, or speed endurance runs of 300m–800m. By now I am supervising Seb's training more closely so that I can start to apply some of the more highly stressing sessions. Such sessions need careful observation of the runner so that they can either be shortened, or longer recovery periods be given (longer recovery may also be achieved by adjusting a work load on the subsequent days). From now on, and right through the racing season, no hard and fast schedules can be given as I keep his work under continual review, taking the actual performances in training as a guide to what part of his progress needs advancing or holding back.

Multi-tier training

An example of a typical twelve days' work in the early part of the
year for a top-class athlete

1 Sunday	4 × 1600m or 3 × 2000m	5000m Pace
2 Monday	Fartlek	
3 Tuesday	8 × 800	3000m Pace
4 Wednesday	Road	
5 Thursday	16 × 200m	1500m/1 Mile Pace
6 Friday	Rest if race If not racing – Fartlek	
7 Saturday	Race or Time Trial	
8 Sunday	4 × 400	800m Pace
9 Monday	Road Run	
10 Tuesday	1 × 300, 2 × 200, 4 × 100, 8 × 60 400m Pace	
11 Wednesday	Fartlek	
12 Thursday	Race – or choose pace for next race. (e.g., if next race is 800m, train at 1500m pace; if 400m, train at 800m pace; if 1500m train at 5000m pace).	

This is not the multi-tier training as advocated by Frank Horwill, but one
modified to Seb's requirements. We believe Horwill's principles to be very
sound, but every athlete should have his or her own schedules.

(One safe generalisation is that three or four times a week there will be an easy morning run of 6.5km to 8km at 3min 20sec to 3min 30sec per kilometre pace.)

There are occasions when we need a time trial to check the level of performance, either generally or in a particular area. These have to be handled with great care, and the coach must have an intimate knowledge of the athlete before he can draw a proper conclusion from the results. For example, Seb performs much better when racing than when training – the opposite can be true for many runners.

Non-running training

Weight Training: Two thirds of the work is repetition lifting in sets of six. One third will be pyramid work to reach a maximum lift. It is all-round weight work; squats, split squats, bench press and curling. Overhead lifting is limited because of the risk to the back. Slim middle-distance runners must seek to perfect their technique if they are to avoid injury.

Circuit Training: As in running, the variables are intensity, duration and frequency which progress simultaneously with the general training. Circuit training is a good time to develop dynamic strength, and bounding exercises, particularly box-jumping, are ideal for developing power. A session of less than one and a half hours is unlikely to allow sufficient variety of exercises or enough time at each station. The great Ron Clarke always said that a runner could not be too strong around the middle, and long repetitions of sit-ups should be included.

Flexibility Exercises: These should be done in any spare time and not restricted to training sessions only. The world-class athlete must be mentally prepared to take every opportunity to protect himself from casual injury. After prolonged study he should get up from his desk carefully, be sure he is warm and bend and stretch carefully. The flexibility exercises for a hurdler are a perfect safeguard.

However, the last two weeks might be as follows, counting down from day 14 to day 1.

Days 14–8: might be spent with an easy run of 4–5 miles each morning, with an 8-mile run at a fair pace (5min 40sec per mile) on *Day 9*: Afternoons would be speed training on the track with sets of repetition runs at distances from 80m to 400m. One of these days, perhaps *Day 8*, could be the day of travel.

Day 7: 4 miles easy in the morning and, say, two sets of 3 × 400m in the afternoon.

Day 6: 4 miles easy in the morning and speed drills in the afternoon.

Day 5: At any time during day, an easy jog of 20–30 minutes, and only flexibility exercises.

Day 4: (Heat) Jog in the morning – race in the afternoon or evening.

Day 3: (Semi-final) Jog in the morning – race in the afternoon or evening.

Day 2: Total rest, or a little jog and stretch.

Day 1: (Final) Jog in the morning – Race in the evening.

Throughout the whole period, sound sleep is essential for mental and physical recovery.

Running for one's country in international events at home and abroad, in addition to competing in some of the big European meetings, involves lost time in travel that can be ill afforded. And absence from work or study, which has to be acounted for, adds to the total stress of competition. The ordinary trials and tribulations of work and family life take on an extra dimension for the class athlete. It is very difficult to perform consistently at this level, a point worth remembering when you read reports which cast all their judgments in terms of success or failure.'

For most runners, this sort of training schedule would be frightening. How does Seb face the prospects of the hard training months each year?

'Brendan Foster once described the life of a top-class athlete as "feeling tired all the time", and I thoroughly agree. Tiredness is the commonest symptom of stress for any runner, and there are times that I get home from a hard evening training session when all I want to do is slump into a chair and stare at the wall.

But the days from late spring to mid-summer, when I'm working my body as hard as I can, are something of a challenge too. If the training programme is going well, and I'm meeting my targets, and Peter is satisfied with my progress, the training can be exhilarating, however hard it is. I can wake up in the morning, and it's grey outside and it's starting to rain, and I know I've got to run six fast 800 metre repetitions and that my head's going to be buzzing at the end of them and that I'm going to be shattered by the evening, but I'd far rather do that than face the ordeal of walking round a department store to get the shopping.

I'm very much an "evening man" when it comes to the hard training. I far prefer the sessions in the afternoon or early evening, and I certainly wouldn't want them before 10.30 or 11 in the morning – I'm hardly alive before then. Ideally, I'd always prefer to race in the evening too, the best time for me is between 8 o'clock and 10 o'clock.

It isn't all hard work, day in and day out. I'm lucky in that I can compartmentalise my life to some extent. Many of my friends are not athletes, and those that are don't want to talk about running all the time. So I can switch off mentally from pace charts and lap times for most of the day. This, I'm sure, helps me concentrate better when I really have to – at the end of a hard session when I'm forcing myself to maintain style and pace and momentum even if my instincts are telling me to stop. I always seem to be able to keep in the back of my mind the thought that if the session goes well the preparation will have been that much better and the next target will be that much easier. It's all one more stepping stone to the next achievement.

Sometimes, even in the hardest sessions, there is time to take stock and adapt the training so that it works even better – that makes the toil even more satisfying. I remember a session in Italy last spring when Peter had planned a tough series of forty consecutive 200 metres repetitions at 30 seconds each with short recoveries between them. I had done about twenty of them, and I found that I had been running them faster than we had planned, about 27 seconds each, so Peter cut the total to thirty: we agreed that I had done the required work, things were going well, and an extra ten would prove nothing, only make me more tired. That seemed to me a good example of athlete and coach working well together even when training was at its most exacting. It's often just as vital for a coach to ease up an athlete during these hard months as it is to speed him up.

The best part of these heavy training months are the races themselves – they really do come as a relief. It's never good to feel completely divorced from competition, and it's like a breath of fresh air to break the monotony, wind down for a day, have a race and sharpen up the mind. That's why I've always been keen to have a few indoor races each winter. A good race proves things are going well, and the occasional bad race can always help to highlight some weakness that may have been missed. And frankly, racing is a darned sight easier than training.'

Pace Chart

In training, as well as in racing, pace judgment and pace maintenance are crucial. The accompanying chart indicates accumulated steady-pace times

Miles 1	2	3	4	5	6	8
mins secs					hrs mins secs	
4 40	9 20	14 00	18 40	23 20	28 00	37 20
4 50	9 40	14 30	19 20	24 10	29 00	38 40
5 00	10 00	15 00	20 00	25 00	30 00	40 00
5 10	10 20	15 30	20 40	25 50	31 00	41 20
5 20	10 40	16 00	21 20	26 40	32 00	42 40
5 30	11 00	16 30	22 00	27 30	33 00	44 00
5 40	11 20	17 00	22 40	28 20	34 00	45 20
5 50	11 40	17 30	23 20	29 10	35 00	46 40
6 00	12 00	18 00	24 00	30 00	36 00	48 00
6 10	12 20	18 30	24 40	30 50	37 00	49 20
6 20	12 40	19 00	25 20	31 40	38 00	50 40
6 30	13 00	19 30	26 00	32 30	39 00	52 00
6 40	13 20	20 00	26 40	33 20	40 00	53 20
6 50	13 40	20 30	27 20	34 10	41 00	54 40
7 00	14 00	21 00	28 00	35 00	42 00	56 00
7 10	14 20	21 30	28 40	35 50	43 00	57 20
7 20	14 40	22 00	29 20	36 40	44 00	58 40
7 30	15 00	22 30	30 00	37 30	45 00	1 00 00
7 40	15 20	23 00	30 40	38 20	46 00	1 01 20
7 50	15 40	23 30	31 20	39 10	47 00	1 02 40
8 00	16 00	24 00	32 00	40 00	48 00	1 04 00
8 10	16 20	24 30	32 40	40 50	49 00	1 05 20
8 20	16 40	25 00	33 20	41 40	50 00	1 06 40
8 30	17 00	25 30	34 00	42 30	51 00	1 08 00
8 40	17 20	26 00	34 40	43 20	52 00	1 09 20
8 50	17 40	26 30	35 20	44 10	53 00	1 10 40
9 00	18 00	27 00	36 00	45 00	54 00	1 12 00
9 10	18 20	27 30	36 40	45 50	55 00	1 13 20
9 20	18 40	28 00	37 20	46 40	56 00	1 14 40
9 30	19 00	28 30	38 00	47 30	57 00	1 16 00
9 40	19 20	29 00	38 40	48 20	58 00	1 17 20
9 50	19 40	29 30	39 20	49 10	59 00	1 18 40
10 00	20 00	30 00	40 00	50 00	1 00 00	1 20 00

for distances from two miles to a full marathon, with the minutes-per-mile times in the left-hand column.

10	12	Half-Marathon 13m 193y	15	20	Marathon 26m 385y
46 40	56 00	1 01 11	1 10 00	1 33 20	2 2 21
48 20	58 00	1 03 2	1 12 30	1 36 40	2 06 44
50 00	1 00 00	1 05 33	1 15 00	1 40 00	2 11 06
51 40	1 02 00	1 07 44	1 17 30	1 43 20	2 15 28
53 20	1 04 00	1 09 55	1 20 00	1 46 50	2 19 50
55 00	1 06 00	1 12 06	1 22 30	1 50 00	2 24 12
56 40	1 08 00	1 14 17	1 25 00	1 53 20	2 28 34
58 20	1 10 00	1 16 28	1 27 30	1 56 40	2 32 56
1 00 00	1 12 00	1 18 40	1 30 00	2 00 00	2 37 19
1 01 40	1 14 00	1 20 51	1 32 30	2 03 20	2 41 41
1 03 20	1 16 00	1 23 02	1 35 00	2 06 40	2 46 03
1 05 00	1 18 00	1 25 13	1 37 30	2 10 00	2 50 25
1 06 40	1 20 00	1 27 24	1 40 00	2 13 20	2 54 47
1 08 20	1 22 00	1 29 35	1 42 30	2 16 40	2 59 09
1 10 00	1 24 00	1 31 47	1 45 00	2 20 00	3 03 33
1 11 40	1 26 00	1 33 58	1 47 30	2 23 20	3 07 55
1 13 20	1 28 00	1 36 09	1 50 00	2 26 40	3 12 17
1 15 00	1 30 00	1 38 20	1 52 30	2 30 00	3 16 39
1 16 40	1 32 00	1 40 31	1 55 00	2 33 20	3 21 01
1 18 20	1 34 00	1 42 42	1 57 30	2 36 40	3 25 23
1 20 00	1 36 00	1 44 53	2 00 00	2 40 00	3 29 45
1 21 40	1 38 00	1 47 04	2 02 30	2 43 20	3 34 07
1 23 20	1 40 00	1 49 15	2 05 00	2 46 40	3 38 29
1 25 00	1 42 00	1 51 26	2 07 30	2 50 00	3 42 41
1 26 40	1 44 00	1 53 37	2 10 00	2 53 20	3 47 13
1 28 20	1 46 00	1 55 48	2 12 30	2 56 40	3 51 35
1 30 00	1 48 00	1 58 00	2 15 00	3 00 00	3 56 00
1 31 40	1 50 00	2 00 11	2 17 30	3 03 20	4 00 22
1 33 20	1 52 00	2 02 22	2 20 00	3 06 40	4 04 44
1 35 00	1 54 00	2 04 33	2 22 30	3 10 00	4 09 06
1 36 40	1 56 00	2 06 44	2 25 00	3 13 20	4 13 28
1 38 20	1 58 00	2 08 55	2 27 30	3 16 40	4 17 50
1 40 00	2 00 00	2 11 07	2 30 00	3 20 00	4 22 13

Running Into Trouble and Out Again

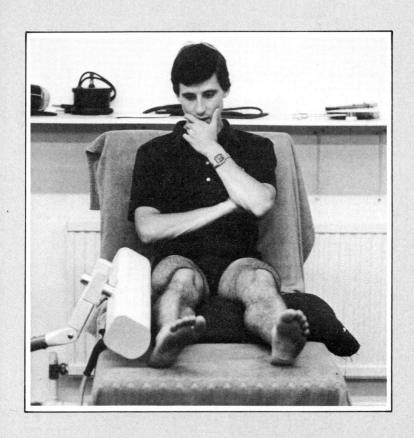

No training programme ever goes *absolutely* to plan. At whatever level you are running, you are deliberately putting extra strain on your body, and if you are competing, whatever the standard, you are putting unaccustomed pressures on your mind as well. Muscles do get strained, feet do sometimes hurt, runners catch cold just like everyone else, and, just like everyone else, they sometimes lose concentration.

An ache or a persistent niggle can hold up your training programme for a day or two; an illness or a bad injury can put you out of action for weeks, and throw a well-conceived training programme into total confusion. It is important for any runner to know what is serious and what is not, and very convenient if he has some idea of how to treat the minor things that might go wrong.

THE FEET

If your feet let you down, you really *have* had it. For no other part of the body is the saying 'prevention is better than a cure' more appropriate, and proper care of the feet will pay back a runner many, many times over.

With feet the first rule of body care particularly applies – keep them clean. Hands get washed several times a day, mainly because they are visible and therefore attract attention. Feet, which are structural marvels, are out of sight and so ignored. Yet although they are normally covered up they can pick up a lot of dust and dirt during a day.

Don't wait for pain, examine your feet regularly. Trim toenails square, look for corns starting and the build-up of calluses. Some toughened areas of skin must be expected, and indeed do offer some protection, but if they are allowed to become too thick they create very painful pressure points and damage the soft tissue underneath. A blister under soft skin is not difficult to treat but a blister under a thickened and toughened patch can become serious, so keep down the thickness of hard skin.

Fashion shoes, male and female, are a menace. The heels are invariably too high, and have the effect of shortening the calf muscles. One American podiatrist recommends running shoes with heels as high as or even higher than everyday walking shoes, to take the strain off the back of the legs. There are not many running shoes, if any, with heels as high as contemporary male fashion would dictate. Better to use everyday shoes with low heels.

Be aware of your own shape. If you are even slightly knock-kneed you are placing an extra strain on the inside of the foot; if you are bow-legged you will have an outside-edge foot-strike with an extra twist (pronation) on landing. Being aware of these conditions can help you with shoe choice and the selection of inserts, though if you do need orthotics you should seek professional advice.

Help your feet by doing regular leg-stretching exercises. Can you comfortably touch your toes? Tightness in the calves reduces ankle flexibility, and this is often the start of tendonitis. Regular exercises to strengthen the feet provide an excellent injury prevention, especially for beginners.

After bad sprains the tendons are restored along with muscle tone, but the ligaments, which are the clever, intricate strappings that bind the foot together, are another matter. Strains weaken a foot and if great care is not taken, the foot becomes progressively more vulnerable and strains more frequently.

Exercising on a wobble board, rolling a ball or bottle around under the foot, sitting and rotating the foot to the maximum, repeated heel raises, gripping and holding with the toes, and walking around barefoot on carpet on the extreme edges (inside and outside) of the foot are all examples of what you can do to build up their strength.

Foot sores

Localised pressure that becomes too intense will form calluses, and rubbing that generates heat can produce soreness and blisters. Both problems can be alleviated by padding and taping. But general advice is difficult to give, because if padding and taping is done without expertise it can often result in relieving one problem spot and starting another. People vary in their skin response to prolonged contact with adhesive tape, too, and what might be a useful temporary help to a miler could be bad for a distance runner.

If a layer of plastic skin (now stocked by most specialist chemists) can be built up to an adequate thickness it will provide a sterile protection which does not need removing. In the time it takes to disappear it will have given some protection against all but the most severe work. But the application of the 'new skin' must not be rushed. Each thin, even layer is best dried off with a hair dryer until the required protective thickness is achieved. The effectiveness of this treatment is limited by the severity of the blistered patch.

Blisters

First of all, make sure that your shoes are a good fit, and do not run in worn-out shoes – keep them in good repair.

If you do get blisters, leave any small ones alone, but try to identify the irritation that caused it. If this is removed the blister will probably be absorbed.

If the blister is big and painful, first clean and disinfect the surrounding area thoroughly and relieve the pressure by draining. Sterilise a needle and insert it horizontally into the edge of the blister and allow the fluid to escape. Do not cut or tear the skin – leave it covering the blister. By inserting the needle this way you avoid piercing the soft tissue and causing bleeding.

After drawing the blister, again clean the area with an antiseptic and dust with a suitable foot powder. If the skin seems very delicate, cover it with a tape, but make sure that the adhesive area is not on the loosened skin; if it is, it may pull the skin away when it's removed. Leave the tape until some new skin has formed under the old.

If under hard or racing conditions you break through the thickened skin and get a raw surface which bleeds, your foot needs very careful treatment. Soccer players frequently place a full strapping of adhesive tape right round the foot and over the bare wound. The sensitive soft tissue underneath is thus protected, and since the adhesive is in contact, slipping and rubbing cannot take place.

The obvious hazard in this procedure is that soccer players, especially pros, play from game to game, but runners have to think further ahead than this. If you stick an adhesive to a bare wound any natural skin or protection that might grow is easily removed with the tape – every time you do it.

If you cannot or will not stop running, leave the wound cleaned and, as much as possible, exposed to the air or lightly covered. Then, when you run, lightly cover it with a special non-stick dressing and with broad tape cover the whole area to keep the dressing in place.

Some people advise you to relieve the pressure by sticking pads of chiropodist's felt into your shoes, suitably cut away, or by placing packing along the sides of the shoes. If your shoes are a proper fit this will be difficult, and if it is easy your shoes may be a bad fit, which probably triggered the blister in the first place. When you have run on a burst blister and released fluid, which will probably have contained blood, remember when cleaning the foot with antiseptic that the now dirty insole of your shoe will also want cleaning.

Finally, whether on track, road or field, and especially if you have run without socks, do not at the end of a run immediately pull off your shoes and walk around for relief. You may have unnoticed scratches on your skin, which could pick up an unpleasant infection.

Athletes Foot

This infection of the foot, usually between the toes, is caused by a microscopic fungus. There are many kinds of application to help cure it though the most effective are those which are most specific to the type of fungus causing the complaint. Even your doctor may have to use trial and error to find the best remedy. There is an antifungal, Griseofulvin, available in tablet form, which can aid in curing forms resistant to local treatment; it is available only on prescription.

Dhobie itch is the same complaint but on a different site, the groin. These ailments should be treated promptly and taken seriously. Go straight to your doctor. Generally, the best prevention is to keep scrupulously clean and dry in these areas. Take care that chafing does not open the skin.

DOUBTS, ACHES AND NIGGLES

Some of the troubles that beset runners are minor – magnified, perhaps, in the runner's mind by the effect they are having on his training, and causing him worry at a time when he doesn't want it. But a few can be 'run through', and with care will disappear without long-term treatment. While it is important to recover from an injury, it is also important to discover the cause, otherwise it will very likely recur on resuming running.

Stress

However much we hear about suspect knees and dodgy achilles tendons, the most common cause of disability for a runner is purely and simply stress, and it remains the most usual reason of all for bad or under-par performance.

Professor Hans Selye's theory is that we all have a fixed stress reserve. There is a reserve tank which is filled with an anti-stress agent, and no matter what the cause of the stress, mental or physical, we draw on the same tank to meet these demands. The logical conclusion from this is that if you are feeling low from overwork, examination worries or personal problems, these worries will be drawing from your anti-stress tank. If the level gets low, a series of heavy training sessions might drain the tank, and you would then begin to show one or more of the typical stress symptoms.

While a combination of various stresses may get you run down quickly, any one factor, if strong enough, will ultimately have the same effect. This does not contradict the view that a good run in the fresh air and in congenial surroundings is refreshing. It is indeed very good therapy and is a great relief from work stress.

The problem is only the old enemy – excess. When stress becomes excessive, something has to give and you must consider yourself as a whole.

First, check your general health and consider everything from your diet to an infection from a cold, a tooth abcess or a small cut. Check whether your resting pulse rate has increased. Are you sleeping well or are you keeping late hours? Have you gone on to shift work, or begun swotting for examinations? They all count. A sudden and heavy increase in your training load, even if it does not bring on injury, will certainly be stressful.

Any of the following could figure among the symptoms of stress: an unexpected weight loss, the symptoms of a recurring or long-lasting common cold such as a runny nose or sore throat and a nervous sneezing. And don't write off backache merely as driving or bad posture; this too is a sign that you could simply be run down. All these symptoms would almost certainly be accompanied by a diminished performance.

A classic symptom, one that Seb has shown once or twice over the years, is a swelling of the lymph glands, particularly in the groin. Be careful. If swollen glands persist after your training has eased off, and you still feel poorly, consider the possibility of glandular fever (*mononucleosis*) which is thought by some to be stress-induced and which, according to observations in the USA is commonly found among the fittest athletes.

Seb has experienced certain stress symptoms when the training has been going well; the training itself was not excessive, but he was also revising hard for his degree finals. The training was cut back, but the symptoms did not disappear until the exams were over. The bounce back was almost immediate, and only a short while later he broke his first world record, the 800 metres, in Oslo. In simple physical terms, that degree of recovery was just not on.

The subject of stress is very well covered in the chapter 'When Things Go Wrong' in *The Complete Middle Distance Runner*, that excellent book by Watts, Wilson and Horwill.

Of course, not every discomfort you feel is going to be the result of stress. If you suffer from an allergy, like hay fever, you may also be sensitive to bright sunlight. When you first start training and racing on a very bright day, early in the year, you can easily experience a runny nose, sneezing or sore eyes. If these pass off within a day or two they are not stress symptoms – if diagnosis was easy we would all be physicians. Everyone should learn what they can about themselves, not in submission to obsessive hypochondria, but simply to observe what does or does not suit them and, if possible, why.

Stiffness

Muscles well used in endurance work, or enlarged with strength training, tend to shorten, which in turn decreases the range of movement – the flexibility – in the joint. Unless this condition is continually relieved with the proper mobility exercises there is every likelihood that you will suffer from frequent bouts of stiffness.

The veins have a system of non-return valves to prevent blood from pooling in the lower limbs. The rhythmic contraction of the muscles alternatively squeezes and releases the veins in the muscles and because of the non-return valves the returning blood is urged towards the heart.

During hard work there is an increase of body fluid diffused throughout the muscle tissue which needs to be reabsorbed and flushed away by the returning blood. A sudden cessation of work stops this auxiliary pumping action and can leave some of the by-products of muscular work still in the tissue. This causes stiffness. So another precaution is properly tapering off at the finish of a training session. Prolonged or persistently uncomfortable stiffness can be relieved by massage.

Massage principally assists the return flow of blood and lymph by its rhythmic action. The pressure stroke on the muscle is always towards the heart. Massage also relaxes the muscle and dilates the surface blood vessels, which helps to restore a feeling of comfort and well-being. The application of heat, too, either by radiant heat or warm baths, also dilates the blood vessels, and can be very relaxing and soothing.

A variation on this heat treatment, which is often used specifically on the lower leg for tendonitis, is the alternate application of heat and cold. This promotes a significant increase in circulation, and it is believed to give relief through the vigorous flushing out effect by the blood. This hot and cold method seems to be more effective with younger people.

Take care when using rubifacients – any of the 'heat creams', for example. These creams dilate the blood vessels locally, and the increased blood supply brings warmth to the area and gives a sense of comfort and relief. But read the instructions carefully, especially about the degree of rubbing in or massage. It is best to make a test application to a small area of skin and look at the reaction. Seb finds the reaction to certain creams very fierce, sometimes accompanied by swelling.

With generalised stiffness – as long as it has not been brought on by injury – it is always best to maintain as wide a range of movement as you can without aggravating the soreness, and a good old soak in a hot bath is fine. Some soreness in muscles, though, is caused by tears in the fibres. The severity of these minute tears will determine to what extent you can carry on training.

The Stitch

The exact nature of the stitch is uncertain but it can be a sign of not being fit enough for the job in hand. When, on two occasions some years ago now, Seb had a bad stitch, they came on in cross-country races early in the year. They both came after very fast starts, and pointed to lack of training for that intensity of running.

If the stitch is slight, it is possible to run slowly through the discomfort and continue the race, by easing up and inclining the body towards the pain. But if it is severe and continuing, you must stop. A prolonged muscle spasm leaves you with a painful bruised feeling which can last for several days. That said, it is much better to be fit enough for the race than to learn how to run through the stitch.

Cramp

The exact cause of cramp associated with running is very uncertain.

Cramp is the everyday word for a painful muscle spasm. When the attack is induced by excessive sweating or heat stroke from exertion in hot conditions it is often due to a lack of salt, for which the only cure or prevention is an adequate salt intake. Other cramps can be caused by an interruption of the blood supply such as a diversion of the blood from the stomach to working muscles particularly if the exertion is too close to a heavy meal.

The simplest remedy for these painful muscle contractions is, wherever possible, to stretch the affected muscle. This may need someone's assistance, because some 'locked' muscles, such as those in the thigh or the calf are very powerful indeed.

Can Massage Help?

The position of massage in sport is not a simple one. While it has specific physiological functions, it often has a psychological one too. Massage can be compared with the excessive and incorrect warm-up routines that are adopted by some athletes; the only good they do is to serve as a mental prop, one that makes them feel more secure because they have always done it. In fact, massage incorrectly timed or incorrectly applied can do a lot more harm than the wrong kind of warm-up.

If you do require massage, choose a masseur with all the care with which you would choose a physiotherapist or a sports-medicine physician or surgeon.

The immediate effects of massage can be quite different. They range from a feeling of well-being to one of feeling badly used. To appreciate the latter you would need to have experienced the deep massage that is practised more frequently in some parts of Europe, where you feel the next day almost as if you have been beaten up, only to feel marvellously fresh and fit two days later. This does not mean that any massage that is painful is a good one. Generally it should promote pleasant feelings in the limbs. So it follows that the effects from such a range of feelings could be damaging if wrongly applied. Although the principles are relatively simple, correct diagnosis and correct application take years of intelligent experience.

Massage is used in the treatment of muscle stiffness, including cramps and spasms, deep bruising and inflammation. This is effected by stretching tissue, stimulating the circulation and dispersing fluid, and is carried out by stroking, kneading and striking.

Anyone going for massage should take care that their skin is as clean as possible around the area to be treated in order to avoid skin infections. The lubricant to avoid skin burn will be selected by the masseur.

It cannot be too strongly stressed that massage is much more specialised than just a rub down. The proper dispersal of fluids needs great skill, as does the 'freeing' of tissue after scarring or where a small nerve may be trapped, and the masseurs must know what they are doing.

However, where muscles have stiffened after prolonged exertion and relief is needed, or where ordinary flexibility exercises are either painful or are not working effectively, then proper massage can be very helpful.

As a safety measure before explosive exertions, too, massage has its place, providing the muscles are not overstimulated: overstimulation has the effect of a depressant – exactly the opposite result from the one you are seeking.

ILLNESS AND INJURY

Minor aches and pains, stitches and stiffness can, almost literally, be taken in your stride. A more important decision must be taken by the runner, though, when things have clearly become more serious than that. In times of illness or genuine injury, the runner's response could affect the rest of his running year – or the rest of his career.

The Three Rules of Injury

1. Treat all injuries as serious. This could prevent minor injuries becoming major ones, and serious injuries becoming very serious ones with the need for long lay-offs and drastic cures.
2. If in doubt – _don't_.
3. Begin treatment immediately – a good defence against the possibility of the acute becoming chronic.

Together, these rules are in line with our philosophy of balanced restraint as a guard against an excess either of enthusiasm or, on the other hand, of rationalised sloth. (The latter should be noted by anyone tempted to misinterpret rule two as meaning 'Don't train if you don't feel like it'; training, like diet, has to be maintained to be effective – if you're tempted to give in, just think of the effort that has gone before and ask if you really want to throw it all away.

Illness

Illnesses should be regarded as injuries, and our second rule on injuries holds good here – 'If in doubt – don't'. In our experience, running through an infection does not work. In fact, you don't run through it, because you will feel even worse for trying and eventually you will have to stop as the aches in the joints become even more painful.

Runners who take general care of themselves, maintaining a good diet and regular running in all weathers, will be healthier than those who do not exercise. And unless they are performing at a high level where stress-induced illnesses are more likely, they will be generally more resistant to the common ailments than the rest of the population. So if you are down or going down with something or other the chances are it is not slight, so treat it with respect. Colds, bronchitis, sore throats, any respiratory infections are not helped by rapid breathing through the mouth. Similarly with stomach upsets or any abdominal pain – heavy exertion will not cure them.

Injury

It is always dangerous to oversimplify, particularly for beginners, but it is fairly safe to say that the pain that wears off as you run is not likely to be as serious as the pain that comes on when you run, and the pain you feel continually is certainly the most serious.

For the purposes of this section we will define an athletic injury as one which (a) prevents running, (b) causes any degree of pain while running, and (c) leaves a pain that has been brought on by running. These are principally injuries to the legs, though this leaves a grey area of pain in other areas or organs, the origin of which may not be running even if the onset does occur during running.

Running injuries are mainly those of over-use. Although brought on when running or by running, they are structural injuries, and frequently the result of inherent structural weakness. The injuries of distance men are usually from prolonged repetitions of movements through the same range, seeking out the weakest link in the chain.

Before looking at some common injuries, we should make it clear that it has never been our policy to run through injuries – this is no better than playing Russian roulette with your health. Also, an injury that does not respond to the simple remedies we suggested for it must be referred immediately to at least a good and sympathetic doctor. The proper place for accurate diagnosis and treatment is a sports medicine centre, or a doctor with a genuine interest in sports medicine. A good physiotherapist is invaluable if he or she has direct sports-injury experience and is not dealing mainly with the everyday infirm; the better the physios, the more closely they will be working with a good ortho-paedic doctor. In fact the good sport physiotherapist will very likely be in touch with the best doctors to deal with sportsmen.

The following table is from a *Runners World* survey in which 800 runners, nearly all of them distance men, reported injuries which made them *stop* running. The survey does not indicate whether or not more than one injury per runner was recorded, though this is very likely. These are listed in the order of the frequency with which they occurred.

See table overleaf:

Knees	17.9%	Calves	3.6%
Achilles tendons	14.0%	Heels	3.0%
Shin splints	10.6%	Hips	2.6%
Arches	6.9%	Hamstrings	2.6%
Ankles	6.4%	Thighs	1.3%
Foot fractures	3.6%	Leg fractures	1.0%

The ICE Treatment

I.C.E. are the initial letters of the principal steps taken when dealing with injuries, particularly the traumatic kind: Ice (applied to check any internal bleeding); Compression (to prevent fluid gathering round the site of the injury); Elevation (to take the load off the limb). In the absence of a refrigerated cold pack or an ice-bag, cold water compresses, or even holding the injury under a cold tap, can help. Be careful with the cold packs or ice-bags – the skin should have a protective smear (we use olive oil) to prevent skin burns or skin sticking to the frozen pack. And crush the ice before it goes into the ice-bag, so that it can conform to the limb contours more easily than can big cubes from the refrigerator.

Knees

Knee injuries are quite often the result of some biomechanical weakness. Runners who already play a sport like soccer, where the continual twisting and turning in studded boots tends to anchor the foot to the ground, must be careful. Any knee injury due to football will be found out in continuous running.

The knee has thirteen ligaments to keep it in position, but it also depends upon the strength of the thigh muscles. Strong muscles and good muscle tone generally helps with the stability of joints. *Chondromalacia patella* is the technical name given to certain kinds of painful knee. The pain occurs behind the kneecap usually accompanied by grating – if the hand is placed over the kneecap while the knee is being flexed the underlying roughness can be felt and even heard.

This is due to a breakdown of the normally very smooth and slick surfaces. The kneecap (*patella*) protects the front of the joint and increases the leverage of the quadriceps extensor muscle so that it presses into the groove at the end of the femur when the leg is straightened. Obviously if it moves to one side because of muscular weakness or structural imbalance or both, the increased friction will wear the sliding surfaces unduly. Consult an orthopaedic specialist or podiatrist and have your feet examined. Very often the correctly designed orthotic will prevent further trouble.

Cortisone injections and surgery have been tried in past years without much success, and surgery is by no means a certain cure. The treatment recommended is isometric exercise to strengthen quadriceps, ice to reduce swelling at onset, and elevation to reduce the weight load. It is one of those pains which can be caused by running on sloping surfaces, like the sides of hills or road cambers. Finding the cause is the most important thing here.

Cartilage
Cartilage is a specialised form of connective tissue which is firm but flexible and elastic. It is found mainly as spacers between joints (backbone and joints) or the rib ends where the rib cage needs flexibility for expansion. But in common usage it is nearly always used to refer to the semi-lunar discs in the knee joint. There are protective discs between the femur and the tibia, where the joint slides. These can be torn if the knee is severely twisted, and often a torn piece can become detached and lodged in the joint. The knee can become locked with pain and swelling. Immediate treatment is our old friend ICE. This injury requires surgery, but with modern techniques the operation is precise and neat, without the old long incisions.

The Collateral Ligaments
Here the pain is felt in the side of the knee, and without proper treatment the pain will continue for months or, depending on your age, even years. If the leg is kept straight, is restrained above the ankle and the knee pushed gently inwards, any pain might indicate damage to the medial ligament, the pain being felt on the inside of the knee. If, when the procedure is reversed and the knee is eased outwards, pain is felt on the outside of the knee, this could be the lateral ligament.

Complete rest, not just from running, is indicated if you are to avoid a long-lasting disability. Small tears will clear up with immobilisation and rest, but larger tears may require surgery.

Achilles Tendon

This is the tendon connecting the calf muscles to the heel. It slides in a loose protective sheath which is slippery internally. If, through excessive rubbing, the lubrication breaks down, the sheath becomes sore and inflamed (*tendonitis*). (It can, more rarely, become inflamed through rheumatism or infection.) If the sheath becomes so inflamed that it swells, and so constricts the movement of the tendon even more, the condition becomes serious, and combined with the small lesions in the tendon it can eventually produce a total seize-up in the tendon sheath. This can only be cleared away with surgery. The condition is made worse by continuing to run instead of resting; the repeated running keeps up the tiny internal tearing.

A sudden onset is best dealt with by ICE. Stop weight-bearing and apply cold compresses or an ice-bag for twenty to thirty minutes and continue with alternate hot and cold treatments. After treatment maintain some movement by ankle-rotating exercises with the leg raised. Anti-inflammatory drugs can be very helpful with tendonitis, but do not allow the condition to continue without obtaining expert advice, preferably from a sports medicine centre.

Try to prevent its onset by never wearing shoes that put pressure on your heel or the tendon. Never start running very fast sessions without first building up the speed work gradually. Do not run hard in a new pair of shoes, or even an old pair not worn for a long time. Avoid sudden changes of running surface for long runs – for instance, if most of your mileage is done on grass in the local park, do not suddenly run ten or twelve miles on a hard road, or vice versa. Get used to the different surfaces gradually. If any sign of tendonitis occurs, you can take the strain off the tendon by placing heel lifts, preferably spongy ones, in both shoes. But remember to raise both your heels equally, in the unaffected leg as well, to avoid creating an imbalance.

Shin Splints

This is sometimes just called shin soreness. Diagnosis is difficult because shin splints can mean anything to anyone so long as the front of the lower leg is sore.

True shin splints is technically *periostitis* of the tibia. This is inflammation of the fibrous coating of the bone, and when it is localised it is not easy for a non-expert to distinguish between this and a stress fracture. The painful area is mainly between the tibia and fibula. The cause of this injury is uncertain – the treatment is to stop running and get physiotherapy as soon as possible. Ultra-sonic treatment and hydrotherapy have all given relief. The do-it-yourself hot and cold treatment is helpful too.

Another form of shin splints is pain in the anterior tibia muscle, the long muscle down the outside of the shin that flexes the foot.

This, too, requires that you stop running immediately, rest for three days and use some form of strapping. Brian Lewis, sometime head track trainer at the University of Indiana, considers this injury to be so varied and complex that the successful treatment requires a variety of taping and support and a great deal of trial and error.

Diagnosis is a real difficulty with shin splints. Some old timers have recommended running through this complaint, which would be wrong even if it did turn out to be only shin splints. But as we said when discussing diagnosis, a localised soreness, which might even spread to a rather larger area, could be an incipient stress fracture. If a runner attempts to run through this pain, he will not emerge from the other side cured; he could go on to develop a full stress fracture which would require a minimum of six weeks' rest before he could start easy training again.

Shin soreness promptly dealt with will not normally last that long. Both kinds of shin splints can be brought on by sudden increases in mileage or even long drives with a foot poised over a foot pedal. Extra attention to careful stretching of the anterior tibia muscle can give relief.

Arches

Not all feet that appear flat-footed actually are. The longitudinal arch may appear to be flat on the floor, but only because the ankle is rolled inwards. A pronated foot will apply a painful twisting force to the ankle with further pain in the knee, even reaching as far as the lower back.

Although the function of an arch is to support weight, the ends of the arch must be fixed for it to do this. In the human foot the ball is connected to the heel by the *plantar fascia*. This strong ligament acts as a tie bar, but it is vulnerable to bruising at the attachments – runners with very high arches are more prone to this condition.

The rear attachment of the fascia is on the base of the heel bone (*calcaneum*), and it is here that some runners feel pain. At first it feels just like a bruise but if you ignore it the pain gets worse and the heel becomes deeply inflamed. Physiotherapy may assist recovery, and relief from soreness may be obtained by fitting soft inserts in the heels, with the centre cut out to relieve pressure under the heel (also a good treatment for bruising on this part of the foot).

Sometimes damage to muscles and other tissues gives rise to spontaneous deposits of calcium and this can happen here. If calcium is deposited it can turn into a heel spur. A similar condition can arise at the back and on top of the heel where, if it continues, the spur may cut into the achilles tendon – a painful and dangerous complaint. Surgical removal is necessary if the pain continues too long.

A bump on the back of the heel can also be a sign, too, that the bursa (see Bursae, below) has also become inflamed. After rest, the only lasting treatment for runners is to have properly fitted supports in the shoes.

Another way to relieve the plantar fascia of some of the strain is to tape the foot so that the ball of the foot and the heel are tied. This needs skilled knowledge, and is a better prevention than cure. If the cause is not attended to, the injuries will always continue.

Pain in the bones of the arches – particularly on the instep – is often the sign of osteo-arthritis, which will be accompanied by some inflammation. This is not too painful except when walking or running. Consult a physician for an anti-inflammatory drug, but osteo-arthritis is a wear-and-tear disease about which little can be done in the long-term. (See also our note on drugs, page 140.)

Ankles

Ankles are easily sprained by rolling the ankle outwards. A strain is a small tear in the muscle or tendons, a sprain is the same thing in a ligament. The injuries are not too serious if treated promptly with ICE and, if possible, an x-ray check to see that no bones are broken.

Rehabilitation has to start as soon as possible. Proper strapping, expertly applied, can restrict movement of the ankle sideways to allow the tear to heal, while allowing some controlled bending and straightening fore and aft. With luck you will be able to resume careful movement in two or three days, and training in less than a fortnight.

It is worth emphasising that prompt and proper treatment is essential, and also that unless any bone is shown to be broken, the ankle should in no circumstances be bound rigid.

One of Seb's rare impact injuries proved a perfect example of how – and how not – to confront a sudden ankle injury. During training on campus at Loughborough he was unlucky enough to thrust his foot down an old grassed-over post hole. The result was very painful and frightening and, with only a few weeks remaining before the 1978 European Championships, very worrying. Seb just sat on the grass stunned with the pain watching his ankle expand like a balloon.

The hospital's first instinct was to put his leg in a plaster. The treatment would not have been wrong – for anyone, that is, except an athlete. Luckily he was rescued in the nick of time and reached the haven of a *sports* physiotherapist who was able to reduce the swelling and strap the ankle in such a way that with additional treatment he was able to resume limited training in less than a fortnight and, in the Championships, win a medal.

This emphasises the importance of finding a sports medicine centre or a doctor interested in sports injuries, or finding an out-patients casualty department where the staff understand and are sympathetic to sportsmen's problems. Every club secretary worth his or her salt will know the nearest centre with a sports medicine facility.

Foot Fractures

These come in two forms. The first is an imbalance and over-use symptom and like stress fractures in the tibia and fibula, it needs no special treatment except rest. Small traumatic breakages, say in a toe after kicking a bed or chair leg, may only require strapping to the next toe. But by and large bones are so strong, and forceful breakage requires such violence, that a doctor should be consulted immediately, not only to supervise the correct setting, but also to check for the associated damage expected from great force. Ice and elevation are in order, but not the movement necessary for compressions: a bad break should not be manipulated before it is properly examined.

Stress Fractures

Stress fractures or hairline fractures are very fine cracks without displacement at the break. This type of fracture is often incomplete, and has not gone right through the bone, though continued use can cause a complete break. Sometimes called march fractures (from continuous heavy marching), they are not easy to diagnose since they do not show on x-ray plates for at least two weeks after onset, when some slight local thickening shows round the crack as repair progresses.

Six weeks' rest from running is the usual requirement. A dietary precaution is to take extra vitamin C to assist healing. Always take medical advice.

As a preventive, avoid running on slopes, either along sides of hills or road cambers. Do not do high speed work on unyielding surfaces, or increase your work load suddenly. Runners in their teens seem to be more prone to stress fractures, even on a good diet. However, check the diet for possible calcium deficiency at any age.

Calves

The calves are very strong sets of muscles, and with foot care and regular stretching they should not give you much trouble if you take care to avoid too much hard running on steep hills, especially in cold weather, and too much sprinting or speed work without experience or warm-up. Runners who have a fore-foot strike certainly place a heavier load on their calves, and while they are proportionately more developed in this area, running on slippery surfaces places more strain on them.

Distance running tends to harden and shorten calf muscles, which tighten the achilles tendons. This in turn means you should always do regular careful stretching exercises.

For general muscle tenseness and soreness a hot bath will bring relief, and general stretching, as well as easing up on distance running, is indicated.

If you have a real muscle pull, which is some degree of tearing to the muscle fibres, the treatment, once again, is ICE. Maintain elevation as much as possible for the first one or even two days. While resting the leg keep tensing the quad muscles and keep rotating the foot. Muscles lose tone quickly, and stiffness should be avoided.

All muscle tears mend with scar tissue. Subsequent exercise must be resumed with care because scars are not elastic like the rest of the muscle tissue.

Heels See under Arches.

Hips

Aches around the hips are usually just strain from long mileage – more often from cross-country runs – and rest is the simple cure, together with reduced mileage. However, many people have one leg just a little shorter than the other, or run habitually on one side of the road, both of which cause the hips to tilt to accommodate the difference. A fallen arch on one foot only can have the effect of shortening that leg. Steady running with its repetitive movements will seek out any imbalances of this kind, and could well result in pain in the lower back. If you have not slipped or fallen and the onset of hip pain is gradual, consider any of the above causes. The remedy is probably foot care.

Hamstrings

These are the powerful muscles at the back of the thigh. If the tear is slight it may be difficult to locate and may only cause stiffness the next day. On the other hand, if a sharp stabbing pain or even a snap is felt, there will be quite a lot of pain at once.

Tears in muscle fibres are always accompanied by tears in blood vessels, so there will be some internal bleeding. The treatment is ICE, and the ice should be applied for twenty minutes, three or four times a day; the leg should be elevated for forty-eight hours. The compression bandage should be of the ACE type (see below under Thighs).

The rehabilitation programme should be undertaken slowly and carefully, and never rushed. Depending on the severity of the tear, a gentle stretching programme may be commenced after two days.

A mild pull can be left to your own care, but any hamstring pull accompanied by great pain or severe limping should have professional advice as soon as possible from a physiotherapist or a doctor.

Thighs

Injuries to the tops of the thighs or the groin are limiting strains mainly brought on by slippery surfaces. The adductor muscles pulling the legs in are often under sudden strain if the foot tries to slip sideways. Normally rest is a sufficient cure with gentle flexing exercise of the knees when lying down.

Do not do squats in weight training, and continue flexibility exercises only with great care.

Pulled muscles in the front of the thigh are often more severe than hamstrings, especially in the belly of the *rectus femoris*. These are more a speed merchant's complaint, and are infrequent in distance runners. The treatment, as for the hamstrings, is best effected with an ACE. This is a good compression pack consisting of a large piece of cotton lint that covers the affected area, which has had a liberal coating of analgesic cream. The whole is kept in place by overlapping Elastoplast strips, the ends of which cross on the pad and not on the leg. This is not the easiest dressing to apply yourself, and in any case, injuries of this type should have medical attention.

Leg Fractures

If the break is by force, you are going straight to hospital for treatment and setting anyway.

Leg fractures for runners are usually stress fractures in the lower leg, probably in the lower third of the fibula or even the tibia. Stress fractures do not suddenly go with a snap, and if you recognise the signs you can avoid them developing. The first warning is a localised soreness, more an ache, which starts right over the bone. At first there may be no additional pain with finger or thumb pressure but the site of the injury will soon become more sensitive.

Stop running at once, and completely rest the leg from load-bearing exercise. And don't rush it: whether the bone is cracked or you are only feeling the onset, you are going to have to stop for six weeks.

Check your shoes for extra wear and look for any imbalance. The fibula is a thinner bone and has to take more twisting than the big shin bone, and is more frequently troublesome.

All that we have said about stress fractures earlier applies here. Take care with surface changes, new shoes, old worn ones. A bad foot plant with excessive pronation is a prime source. Favouring an injury, say a blistered foot, on a long run can also bring on a hairline crack.

You may be advised to strap the leg, but our orthopaedic advisers have not considered it necessary, and on both occasions Seb has suffered a stress fracture he has made a complete recovery.

Bursae

These are pockets of fibrous tissue with a slippery lining which are there to reduce friction where tendons or ligaments pass over bones in joints. They can become inflamed from damage, say a sharp blow, or from extra pressure and the inflammation is often accompanied by fluid which causes them to swell. Unless it has been caused by infection, inflammation is usually the result of excessive friction or pressure.

The knees and heels – and sometimes elbows – are the bursae that most worry runners. It is usually best to rest these joints with some compression if there is excessive fluid present, until the inflammation subsides and the fluid is absorbed. Draining is always a risk and seldom recommended – an infection in a joint is always serious.

Bruising

Bruising is caused by damage to the tissue, which releases fluid. Often the very small blood vessels are ruptured and release blood into the surrounding tissue where it gradually decomposes and is absorbed. This process gives rise to the blue and yellow discoloration.

In severe cases the injury can be too painful to treat, but there are useful ointments which can help to reduce inflammation and swelling. This is done not by getting into the damaged tissue directly but by the active constituents being absorbed through the skin into the blood and thus reaching the site of the injuries. These ointments also contain ingredients to reduce stiffness, and they can be useful with sprains. Two such ointments have the trade names Lasonil and Movelat; they are non-greasy and come in tubes.

An occasional phenomenon of bruising is that it may show somewhere other than the site of the injury; thus a blow on the buttocks or thigh might show in the calf. If you can't remember any injury to the discoloured area, think of a knock you might have had somewhere else.

Slight bruising unaccompanied by severe pain can be ignored, and very severe bruising is usually the result of injury serious enough to warrant proper medical attention.

Beware of drugs

Drugs are often administered to alleviate as well as to cure ailments. All drugs have side effects. They have to be strong enough to work, and they will always have some effect on the delicate balance of the body's chemistry. Aspirin can make the stomach bleed; phenylbutazone, a powerful anti-inflammatory drug, will affect the blood cells – take enough and you will become anaemic. The trade-off is always between which is the lesser of the two evils – the symptoms of the complaint or the symptoms of the cure.

We cannot comment from personal experience on the use of hydrocortisone injections, but results with athletes of our acquaintance have varied from useless to disastrous.

There is a swing against the casual use of antibiotics, but these medicines are invaluable in the right circumstances. There is a let-down feeling and a fall off in performance after a course of these drugs which as yet is not fully explained, but may be due to interference with certain body enzymes.

If you can manage without drugs, we would advise you to avoid them.

GETTING BACK TO TRAINING

The time it takes to reach the old level of fitness after a lay-off is different for each person, and it will depend largely on what caused the lay-off.

The most easily avoided lay-off is the holiday. The hot sand, the extra cold beers and the lazy reluctance to swim much – they all have to be resisted. Getting back to form after this entails no more than a bit of extra work, so long as it is steadily taken up. Two weeks in the sun will need two weeks to get back to where you were.

Influenza or any virus infection is another matter. With these illnesses, and any illness accompanied by fever, the utmost caution is necessary. If you have had to have a doctor, and if the doctor has prescribed antibiotics, then your recovery period will be a little longer. There is very frequently an additional feeling of lowered energy and effectiveness – a loss of steam as it were – following a course of antibiotics. Do not try to force the recovery, nor should you ever fail to complete the course prescribed just because you suddenly feel better and want to hasten your return to full training. All you will succeed in doing is to spread strains of the infection which are resistant to the treatment. The doctors will love you for this.

In all attempts to resume training after illness the 'one step forward, two steps back' trap is easy to fall into. There is only one golden rule: the training must progress at a rate that always allows you to finish feeling well – healthily tired perhaps, but still feeling well.

Recovery after athletic injuries will depend upon the type and the amount of exercise you are able to carry out while not running. While you are waiting the necessary six weeks after diagnosing or suspecting a simple stress fracture of the fibula or tibia, aerobic work like swimming should be followed as much as possible. Weight training using a multi-gym or a bench is fine, though using a leg press would be silly. After about two weeks, gentle cycling would also be in order.

After surgery for cartilage trouble you must follow the instructions of the orthopaedic surgeon. If the treatment involved the arthroscopy technique, where only a small hole is made and the pieces are located accurately, the operation is so neat and clean that recovery will be rapid.

But as surgery is invasive, it is also irritating – so give the effects a proper chance to settle down. It is no use having an operation to clean out a seized-up and fouled-up achilles tendon, and then replacing the trouble with another by not allowing the healing to progress quietly.

However, most ailments that runners suffer from are those of over-use, and once these have cleared up with treatment and training can be resumed, all runners will want to return to full fitness as soon as possible. In hastening the return, quite obviously over-use is to be avoided, and here we have found that a modified form of interval training is very useful. Racing is running quickly, and since speed falls off faster than endurance when you are temporarily out of training, some speed work is needed on your return.

Distance training gives long sustained pounding, whereas *modest* speed with *adequate* recovery is less cumulatively stressful. Since it is estimated that only 60 per cent loading is required to maintain condition, as against at least 80 per cent to improve condition, it would seem sensible to stay as generally active as possible during a lay-off, and to stimulate the heart and the muscles with short-duration exercises. Short sessions of 10 x 150m progressing to 12 x 200m, plus short steady runs of about three miles were what we used in the middle of the summer of 1982 when Seb was recovering from stress fracture and para-tendonitis. Of course, these sessions were not flat out, or as fast as normal training, but they should be rather faster than normal running – say 15sec per 100m pace.

The need to immobilise an injury completely is seldom necessary, and you should resume and maintain flexibility in the limb as soon as possible. This not only speeds up recovery, but lessens the risk of injury when you start up again.

Once training is resumed take great care not to favour the injury. If you have badly sprained an ankle do not resume running favouring that foot because you will run unbalanced. The effect is similar to having one leg shorter than the other, the pelvis will be tilted to compensate and the spine becomes misaligned – just the circumstances to start off another injury somewhere else in the body.

If it is too painful to run on properly, it is too soon to train. If you are favouring it because you are frightened to put full weight upon it, then you must nerve yourself to run naturally.

Whether on a lazy holiday or during any lay-off, do not neglect your flexibility exercises – this will reduce the risk of picking up another injury due to stiffness. Even with ankle sprains or after achilles tendon operations, the doctors will tell you to start flexing the ankle as soon as possible.

For competitive athletes, injuries or illness and the subsequent lay-off and climb back to form are in many ways the most testing time of their careers. Apart from the usual ration of aches and strains and a stress fracture in his teens, Seb's career up to the start of 1982 had been comparatively trouble-free. There was that incident back in 1978 when he badly sprained an ankle during a training run at Loughborough, but apart from leaving him with one ankle slightly (and permanently) bigger than the other, that was soon forgotten.

What will never be forgotten is the traumatic year of 1982, a year that followed his astonishing string of broken records in 1981, and which was planned to culminate in a string of titles in the European Championships in Athens and the Commonwealth Games in Brisbane. Seb describes the year himself:

'I suppose the trouble really started in January. The winter training had all been going reasonably well, and then at the end of January I had something the matter with a foot arch, and I was off for three or four weeks under a physiotherapist. I didn't run again till early March, and as soon as I got back to training I think I must have been pushing a bit too hard. Psychologically it's not very good losing a month's running in the winter, because you know that's what you're going to base your summer stuff on.

Anyway, things seemed to be going fairly well, and I ran in the Yorkshire Championships, and had two weeks' training and a 2000 metre race in Bordeaux before the start of the season proper here.

Then, three or four days after I got back from France I was out with a leg injury – it turned out to be a stress fracture at the bottom of my leg. These things take a long time to diagnose, and mine was complicated by some muscle problem in the same area. But a stress fracture it certainly was, and that meant I was out effectively from the beginning of June to the beginning of August – the one period of the year you just cannot afford to dispense with. It's a time when I'm doing all my sharpening work . . . I lost most of my hard repetitions and my speed training.

Even when I eventually got back to training I could never run more than about six miles for fear of bringing on the injury again; so far as endurance was concerned, I was in pretty bad shape.

I got back to racing after two-and-a-half to three weeks' training, and the mental relief at being back seemed to make me race above my level of fitness – I did a 1 min 44.4sec 800 metres in Zurich, and I was just coasting in the final straight. But the basic problem was simple: I didn't have enough background training, and the European Championships were on top of us.

We decided that I had to have some sort of rehearsal for Athens by running three races close together, all the time knowing that I'd be taking out endurance and speed from a very thin background of work. So I had the Zurich race, followed by the Talbot Games and a race in Cologne, and they went pretty well. And then I had that relay at Crystal Palace when the powers that be decreed that everyone who was going to Athens had to turn up and run something. It was a good run, that 4 × 800 metres when we broke the world record. I did 1 min 43.9sec. which was fast, but in retrospect it can't have done me any good. If I hadn't had that behind me I might at least have felt easier in the heats and semi-final in Athens.

When we got to the European Championships we knew we were living very much on borrowed time. Quite apart from my lack of background training I could tell from the way I was reacting to stress. I was tired, I was easily irritable, my throat was sore, my lymph glands were up – all the classic stress symptoms. I got a blister, too, which would normally have been perfectly all right, but now, it seemed an extra frustration. I was mentally and physically running myself into the deck.

The heat and the semi-final of the 800 metres went satisfactorily, but I didn't find them particularly easy; they were very average times, the sort I should normally have been able to put together in one training session.

And the final was one of those occasions you just hope will never happen again. The race had gone reasonably well. I got to the final bend in front, having got rid of most of the field, then I kicked, expecting to take five or six strides out of the closest runners. Instead I only took about two-and-a-half strides. It was a dreadful feeling. I'd done it so many times in a race before and this time it just didn't work − like sticking your foot down on the accelerator and getting no reaction. I was getting further up the straight, but I knew Hans-Peter Ferner was getting closer all the time, and as he drew level with me, there was that haunting, nightmare certainty that there was nothing more, absolutely nothing, that I could give.

I felt awful, ill, after the race. Back in London at the hospital they diagnosed glandular fever. I hadn't got it now, they said, but I had certainly had it quite recently. It could have been shielded a bit in the weeks when I was laid off with the leg injury. I'd been depressed anyway, being out of action with the season slipping by, and I could have missed the symptoms.

I had a series of hospital tests and a long lay-off that autumn. Only by December was I beginning to feel anything like I felt a year before in terms of health and fitness.

When you're sidelined, frustration is the main trouble − not just missing the glory of racing and all that, but the fact that running is a daily habit − and suddenly not being able to do what you have got used to doing every day for so many years is very disturbing.

And when you're at a high level of competition, the very fact that you're not involved is doubly worrying. Everything seems to be moving away from you at an incredible pace, and there's nothing you can do about it. I try to shy away from it all. I don't want to talk athletics. I don't even want to think athletics. All that seems to matter is getting the injury cleared up, and all I think about is the next physio session.

When you can start up again at last, the feelings are strangely mixed. It's wonderful being able to run again, and it's really exhilarating to have the challenge of getting back to racing fitness. But again there's the dreadful fear in the back of the mind that the injury could return, that you're going to end your next training session hobbling back to hospital. It takes perhaps two weeks for the fear to go. Then if you're lucky you're back to normal again.'

Disaster in Athens: defeat by
Ferner, commiseration from Garry Cook

320

The Big Day

So, it's arrived – the day you have been planning for for weeks, perhaps months, or perhaps, if you have a very special talent, for the whole of your running career. It would be a tragedy if something were to go wrong to spoil the day. It might, of course, be just that someone else runs faster than you bargained for – you can't always plan for that. But a lot of pitfalls can be avoided by forethought and by careful planning; if you get these things right, you'll look back on the day with satisfaction however the race went.

You will have wound down your training in the previous few days or weeks, and with luck you will be feeling fully rested.

Get in your solid good night's sleep *two* nights before the race. If you are running on a Sunday it will be Friday night's sleep that will be the most important. On Friday night the week is over, and you can go to bed early and get up late. You will sleep well, and because the race is not tomorrow you won't toss and turn thinking about how it is going to go. On Saturday, or whatever day is the eve of the race, you can do the opposite. The edgy types should stay up a bit, or go out to see friends, so that they will be tired enough to get off to sleep as soon as they are in bed. When you're sleeping you're not worrying.

Circadian rhythms? They are not special beats from the West Indies, they are the cycles that the body passes through each day, and, with a few exceptions, they occur in everyone. The heart rate, the oxygen uptake and the secretion of various hormones all vary – for the lowest values are in the early hours after midnight. The peaks and troughs are different for women. There is evidence that some active people are sensitive to sleeping at unusual or unaccustomed times, so a couple of hours' sleep in the afternoon or early evening can upset these body rhythms and reduce the subsequent performance. So try to stick to a familiar sleep routine.

What have you forgotten?

Something else will have been concerning you on the eve of the big day, especially if you have an early start in the morning. How much are you going to take with you?

Even if this is your first event, you will have been running long enough to have acquired a lot of kit – far more than you are going to need for one race. But allowing for any contingency, from a snowstorm to a lost sock, you are still going to carry a fair amount with you. Make a list as things occur to you during the previous week, and tick it off as you pack your hold-all. Or use the checklist we have devised on page 150.

Your requirements can be divided into four categories: (1) what you wear before your run, (2) what you wear to run in, (3) what you wear or might need after the run before travelling home, and (4) the secretarial stuff, of which your running number is the most important.

Assuming you are not arriving straight from the Lord Mayor's Banquet, you will probably travel to the race in a *tracksuit*, with perhaps a *sweatshirt* underneath and, if it's cold, a *T-shirt* or a *long-sleeved thermal vest* underneath that. You may also be wearing *long johns* or thin *training trousers* under your tracksuit bottoms. You will also want to carry your *rain top* and *rainproof trousers* in case of a wet start, and probably a *hat* of some kind. Some of these can also help out if it turns really cold before the start and you find you want a long-sleeved vest or long trousers to race in. You will be wearing *trainers* or ordinary *walking shoes*.

To change into for the warm-up, and to race in, you'll carry your *vest, shorts, pants, socks* and *running shoes*. In cold weather you may want an *extra T-shirt* on top and a pair of *cotton gloves*. And *vaseline*, perhaps, to rub on your face and legs to prevent chafing. In summer you might want a *sweatband* or *wristbands*, or even a light *cap*.

Now remember, everything you have worn to this point might well have got either wet or sweaty even before the start. So after the race you will be searching your bag for a clean *T-shirt*, clean *pants*, a clean *sweatshirt*, clean *socks*, a *sweater*, perhaps a *windcheater*. Not to mention a *towel*, some *soap, foot powder* and a *comb*.

If you have taken a knock, you might be grateful for your own *first aid kit* (it's a good idea always to carry one, anyway). It should include *crepe bandage, safety pins, Elastoplast*, an *antiseptic* as well as the *vaseline*. And an *ice-pack* taken from the refrigerator before you leave and wrapped in newspaper for insulation. You can buy packs like this in sealed plastic containers – and very useful they can be.

These should suit most runners' needs. A cross-country entrant might have a variety of shoes to choose from once he has had a look at the course, and many are the runners who wished too late that they had brought a spare pair of *shoelaces*, but if you carry most of the above you are likely to be a lender in the changing room rather than a borrower.

Finally, the secretarial stuff. If you have been sent a *race number*, don't forget it; and in case it gets lost before the start (or during the race) memorise your number – it may mean vital points to your team, it may even be the difference between you being allowed to run or not. Bring *safety pins* to attach it to your vest. Bring some *money* for emergencies, a *pen* (not just for signing autographs – you may want to fill out a results envelope which the organisers will post to you when the final placings have been worked out). Bring the *race details* that came with your number, and a *road map* in case you get lost finding the venue. Wear your *watch*.

Getting There

Some of the most important factors determining how and when you should arrive at a race are psychological, and represent a kind of character profile.

The younger athlete who has had the same coach for a long time will certainly have been conditioned by his coach's thinking. If the coach has spotted something in his behaviour pattern that he thinks is inconsistent with a good performance he will have tried to change or eliminate it.

For example, if a runner is the nail-biting, anxious type, is he better off with the crowds with something happening to take his mind off the forthcoming competition, or is he better off out of it, where he can calm down and not get worked up by the others' feelings of expectancy and excitement? If he is away from the other competitors, does he have more time to worry about the coming trial?

To run in
1. Vest
2. Shorts
3. Pants
4. Socks
5. Running shoes

To warm up in
6. Hat
7. Sweatshirt
8. Trousers
9. T-shirt
10. Rain top
11. Rainproof trousers

To change into after run
12. Sweatshirt
13. Trousers
14. 'V' neck sweater
15. Underpants
16. Shoes
17. Windcheater
18. Socks

Extras for running in hot or cold weather
19. Hat
20. T-shirt
21. Training trousers
22. Sweatband
23. Wristbands
24. Gloves

Miscellaneous
25. Vaseline
26. Plasters
27. Race acceptance
28. Race details
29. Pen
30. Map
31. Number
32. Safety pins
33. Comb
34. Towel
35. Hold-all

At the roadside or the trackside or in the changing room there will always be those who are bragging or exaggerating to keep up their own spirits – this sort of thing can affect an impressionable newcomer.

But it is one thing to be away from the mob with a guide and confidant; it is quite another to be on your own, perhaps feeling lost and lonely.

In Seb's early running days we soon realised that running about with other youngsters was not the best preparation, and something always seemed to go wrong with all the big English Schools Championships except the last one, when Seb won the 3000 metres. This was also the one in which we arrived on our own, in our own transport and in our own time, and from this developed an unvarying pattern that we have kept to ever since.

It takes a lot of work to devise the best pattern, and the extra planning might make it a two-day rather than a one-day problem. But the results are worth it.

The anxiety you might be feeling as you arrive for your first race is nothing, of course, to the pressures on the top track stars. You will be spared the expectancy of supporters, the hopes of the whole nation, as well as the attention of newspaper reporters and television cameras.

However, you will also miss some of the small privileges that go with it, like not having to find the start or the changing rooms, or where to get a bath or where to find the numbers – the new breed of British team managers with our international athletes are a hard-working band. But for the run-of-the-mill runner these can be real irritations, and must be allowed for – in terms of time and patience.

Your first few races will seem chaotic, especially road and cross-country races and, most of all, big relays. If in doubt, arrive early – the problem of waiting for the off is not nearly as unnerving and fatiguing as trying to find the venue, change and get to the start in time with the right numbers. Travelling with a team or a coach is great fun and very supportive if you are on time, but again, if in doubt, arrive under your own steam, be sure you know exactly where the venue is and that you have very clear pre-race information and instructions.

The Cross-country Code

For cross-country meetings, a few expert tips might come in even more welcome – the varying terrain and the very informality of the sport can make it all the more confusing for a newcomer.

Unless you have run the course before, get there in plenty of time to jog round it to familiarise yourself with the layout. It will be too late to change your shoes if you have bent the spikes half way round, or selected the wrong type. If you don't know the course, study the map which should be pinned up near the start or near the changing rooms.

We have always looked for a spot with the maximum shelter to warm up in. On bad days you can get worn out trying to raise your temperature if you are too exposed to the weather.

Keep warm to the very last moment. Youngsters in school races eagerly discard coats and tracksuits and hang around for the start which can easily be delayed. Always leave your discarded gear in a waterproof bag at the finish if you don't have a clubmate looking after them all. If it starts to rain during the race you will not enjoy getting into a soggy tracksuit at the finish.

Knowing the course helps you with the start. It is fine to begin slowly and work your way through the field, the old, classic advice, but if at 300 yards from the start the course narrows to single file, by the time you are through the gap you can be so far back in the queue that you will never catch up.

Heat loss can be cruel on some days, particularly in strong, cold winds and rain. A smear of olive oil on exposed skin, light cotton gloves and long-sleeved running vests should all be considered. Experience is the best guide.

The Old Routine

Once the uncertainties of your first competitive race are over, you will readily settle into a routine for all days such as this. On occasions before a big race, Seb has evolved a sequence that hardly ever changes:

First, a good sleep for a couple of hours. Then he is woken up in time to complete the rest of the ritual, which is to shower, shave and change into freshly laundered kit. This is timed so that he can arrive at the warm-up area approximately forty-five minutes before the race. He finds that this routine reduces the pre-race tension considerably. Clearly it is good to sleep and not to worry, but it is equally bad to sleep and upset your body rhythms if you are sensitive to these changes – what suits one athlete might not suit you.

Certainly, this sequence won't even approximate to yours. But whatever it is, stick to it. The warm-up ritual you have evolved is the one that works for you, so do it as usual. The middle of the race is not the time to think 'Did I warm up enough?' If you are inexperienced, then evolve a sound routine as soon as possible – you need all the confidence you can get.

As for food before the race, don't compete on a heavy, fatty meal or with your stomach swilling around with liquid like a hot water bottle.

That switch of blood from the stomach to the muscles, which the body makes whether you want it to or not, can result in severe pain if the stomach has too much in it. The body knows it wants blood in the muscles to run; it will not know you have handicapped it with too much food eaten too late. People are different, but as a general rule allow at least two hours after a modest carbohydrate meal before you run.

Most athletes nowadays drink very little, too, in the two-and-a-half to five hours before a race – just enough to stop them feeling dry-mouthed. Though for races more than seven or eight miles on the road or across country, where dehydration might become a danger, you will find runners drinking much closer to the start.

The Vital Warm-up

The warm-up performs two functions. Primarily it is a physiological requirement before training or competition. Secondarily, it becomes a psychological requirement evolving out of the first.

The main requirement is to raise the core temperature of the body, increasing it by some 2°F (1.1°C) in order to achieve the following:

1. A reduction in internal friction: muscles contract and antagonistic muscles relax better, and therefore faster and with less risk of injury, when warm; pulled muscles are more common when an athlete is cold.

2. A dilation of the blood vessels, bringing more warmth and fuel supply to the muscles.

3. A general increase in the metabolic rate, so that haemoglobin releases oxygen more readily from the blood.

4. An increase in circulation, so that more oxygen gets to the cells.

Raising a quick sweat is not a true warm up, because although the body may be perspiring freely, and the blood, diverted to the skin for cooling purposes, may make you feel warmer, the inner temperature may not have increased sufficiently to achieve those aims. Runners do not want to, nor could they, be continually consulting rectal thermometers to ascertain their increase in core temperature; only personal experience will tell you when your body becomes freer and looser.

As in so many things, twice as much is not twice as good. In high-performance events, particularly those over shorter distances, an excessively long warm up will make inroads into the natural reserves of the body. Any warm-up routine should contain elements in which the full range of racing movement is encountered, and so you should certainly, for example, gradually work up to some fast striding.

The warm-up routine should also contain flexibility exercises, and again we emphasise that these exercises should not be done cold. They are best done not earlier than midway through your routine. And since the warm-up is, as its name indicates, to get you warm, do not stretch and risk muscle or tendon injury until you *are* warm. Your separate flexibility sessions are to enhance your range of movement so that the range which is normal for your sporting activity keeps you well short of injury.

Events like the hurdles seem to have become associated with the most elaborate flexibility routines, but all athletes would benefit by just being able to do them. If only all athletes in all sports were as flexible as schooled ballet dancers. The demands of their long, energetic roles are considerable, combining as they do running, jumping, lifting and even throwing, a kind of combined event requiring extended ranges of movement under load. Seb may be much more flexible than most middle-distance runners, his admiration for his dancing sister contains not a little envy.

The psychological aspect of the warm-up routine is also important. In competition it plays a large part in maintaining confidence and controlling nerves. Arriving late, and not having time to complete the full routine he has developed over the years, can leave an athlete worrying about not being ready to compete. And when he is doing something positive, like concentrating on his warm-up, the performer has less time to dwell upon his forthcoming trial.

Jogging, striding and stretching are the elements of a runner's warm-up, the intensity and duration of which are modified by the time of day and the weather.

Within the stricture of not taking too much out of your reserves, one might summarise by saying: the shorter the event the more intense the warm-up. Clearly the requirements of a 400 metre hurdler are not those of the marathon man, since the former has to have all systems go from the instant the gun fires.

There is a time-lag between the start of a run and the metabolism catching up with energy requirement during which, depending upon how fast the start is, a small oxygen debt will build up. In a long-distance race a slower start can be tolerated, and indeed has a sound physiological basis. But in 5000 metres and even some 10,000 metres races, the result of being too far off the pace from the start can be truly disastrous.

Besides, it takes a very brave and disciplined athlete to hold back until he is ready to increase the pace slowly and steadily until he has pulled back the gap. The problem here is that in a class race the runner may be running on his own for a long time, which is extra tough, physically and mentally.

Every athlete's warm-up routine is different. Seb's pre-race build-up goes something like this:

'I'm usually at my most nervous when I first arrive at the stadium – particularly if I've walked there from the hotel and been part of the expectant crowd looking forward to the evening's athletics.

The warm-up for me has a genuine psychological effect. All the big stadiums have pretty good facilities now – grass areas away from the noise and the lights of the track – and once you are there you can dampen down the nerves. It's good to know, once you've started your routine, that you have somehow got into the first act of the racing evening.

It's a chance to get a glimpse of the other athletes, too. We all seem to be giving each other sideways glances, just to check who's there, perhaps. But really you are concentrating on your own warm-up, you haven't a lot of time

to look at theirs. Even if you did you wouldn't learn much – they're unlikely to be actually limping, or anything like that.

I think some athletes are inclined to over-do the warm-up. It may be nervousness, perhaps, that doesn't let them stop, but I'm quite sure some runners have left their best performances in the warm-up area. You've got to remember that a warm-up is designed principally to warm you up, and if you can add to that a bit of suppleness and freedom of movement there's no need to go on flogging yourself for an hour or hour-and-a-half. Some people have almost completed full training sessions by the time they walk out onto the track.

For an 800 metre race on a reasonably warm evening I would never need more than thirty-five to forty minutes warming up, and only five or ten minutes of that would be hard work – perhaps some fast strides and some speed drills. The sequence I use has taken shape over the years. I didn't sit down and map it out, it has evolved gradually into its present shape and it works mentally and physically for me. It gets me to the start line warm, supple and mentally prepared to do what I've come to do. It goes like this:

Alternatively walk and jog for five minutes or so.

Jog continuously at a slightly faster pace for about another five minutes, slipping in the odd high knee-lift and little burst of fast-cadence short steps, something like a sprinter's speed drill. By now I will be warm enough for stretching.

Static stretch calves and hamstrings, slowly stretching one leg at a time by leaning forward against a wall or stanchion, with the hands, and the leading

leg, being ready to take the weight and control the tension, the rear leg being stretched with the heel firmly on the ground.

Loosen up the neck, shoulders and arms, combined leg and trunk stretching, by alternately placing first one straight leg and then the other, raised nearly horizontal, onto a radiator, chair or low wall, then bending the trunk forward as parallel as possible to the raised leg and placing the head on the raised knee.

Stand legs astride with hands on hips or behind the head, and bend and rotate the trunk.

Follow with a few half squats, remembering the static part – holding each position for 10–15 seconds. I would allow eight to ten minutes for the stretching exercises.

Resume jogging which, as soon as any 'stretched' feeling passes off, turns into steady running. By now I am warmed up.

A set of, say, four fast strides over about 60 metres each.

Jog down for half a minute.

The whole routine is timed to finish as close to the start of the event as possible. I will stay well wrapped up throughout.'

The Day of the Marathon

The day of every race is a big day – but for many runners new to the sport, the day of the marathon you have dreamed about, and towards which you have worked for months, is the big day to beat them all.

It is a day, too, that calls for more forethought and preparation than any race you might have entered during the build-up . . . because if there is one day on which you really do *not* want things to go wrong, this is the day.

The Marathon Diet

You may well have heard about glycogen-loading via a bleed-out diet. Forget it. While this diet trick can certainly help some runners, it takes a couple of tries at least to get it somewhere near right, and to ensure that you are not one of those people it does not suit.

The full bleed-out treatment involves eating a high-protein diet and hard running for a period and then, a few days before the race, switching to a high-carbohydrate diet so that the glycogen-starved body will over-compensate, and from the high-carbohydrate intake convert and store a larger-than-normal stock of glycogen.

One can easily see the effect that a hard run and a drastic diet shift might have on the learner marathoner. The easier way is to switch to high-carbohydrate meals for three days before the race – just plenty of pasta, bread and potatoes.

The Marathon Gear

What we said about foot care (Chapter Seven) is even more relevant for a marathon; and your shoes must be comfortable and protective. It may seem obvious, but we feel it is worth repeating that lightness is not everything; calculating the effort saved by lighter shoes is useless if you cannot finish the race in the super-lights you have chosen on weight alone. It may be a great shoe, but if you can feel a small stone shortly after the start think how you will feel long before the finish.

Are your shoes cool to run in? Blisters are caused by the heat from friction, and even if your shoe fits well, don't add to the heat by footwear that lacks ventilation. A marathon shoe must breathe. And the linings and inner soles must not rub, ruckle or irritate in any way.

There is nothing worse than an almost neurotic runner worrying over all the trivia instead of getting on with the running and toughening himself, but having said that, if there is a case for being ultra-careful about gear it is in the build-up period to your first marathon.

In our schedule there are no fewer than seventeen runs of ten miles or more, and this gives you plenty of time to discover the irritations that linger, and you should have encountered a sufficient variety of weather to answer such questions as: How does your skin stand up to the rain? Do you chafe easily? Is there a seam or some-such on your singlet that rubs?

Women will have some nipple protection from their bras; men who have never thought of problems in that area should be alert for it now. The continued rubbing from the wrong singlet is a problem: it is better to get a running singlet of the right cut, but otherwise use a second-skin type of adhesive cover, or even a plain adhesive strip.

Socks that may seem all right at five miles can irritate at eight miles. They then become painful at ten miles and impossible a little later. Remember that you are going to be moving your arms, legs and torso for four hours of hard work.

Head gear; you haven't forgotten that, have you? Experiment with a hat or cap if you think you will need one. Four hours' exertion in the sun is a trial to be reckoned with.

Marathon Eating and Drinking

Before the race, do not eat later than three hours before the start, and even then not a heavy protein or fat meal. As for drinking, we would suggest about a pint – not more – some half-hour before the start.

Your body's problem today is going to be the fact that it can only store enough glycogen for a modest day's living, so it is going to be looking for another fuel source when the glycogen gets scarce in the course of your marathon. That source is fat, and one suggestion, made by David Costill in *A Scientific Approach to Distance Running* is that drinking two cups of good coffee an hour before the start helps 'the fat cells liberate more free fatty acids', and has been able to extend the time to exhaustion by 19 per cent.

Costill gives one final no-no. Inside the final hour before the start, do not eat or drink anything that has much sugar in it – sweets, ice-cream, dried fruit, honey, soft drinks or even 'athletic' drinks.

During the marathon you will want to drink from time to time, and your training runs of twelve, sixteen and twenty miles should have given you a chance to establish a drinking pattern. In practice you will want about a quarter or a third of a pint every quarter of an hour or so if the day is at all warm.

You will certainly sweat, and a lot of water vapour is lost in the breath; if you lose too much water you will start to dehydrate, and dehydration can lead to overheating. There are now quite a few so-called balanced electrolytic drinks on the market which are meant to maintain the electrolytic balance (i.e. replace the various salts that are lost). However, not all the experts agree on the correctness of their composition. For example, when we lose salt through sweating, it does not leave the body in the same concentration as it exists in the body fluids. We actually lose the water faster than we lose the salt, so the salt concentration in the body is actually increasing as we run. Which calls for extremely careful composition of salt drinks.

Until you have experimented and found something that you know improves your performance, you are probably safer with water.

The Marathon Itself

As for the race itself (and this includes any run of ten miles or more, particularly if it's a warm day), begin at slower than race pace. Hard running at the start rapidly depletes the glycogen in the muscles, and it may never get a chance to build up enough during the race.

It is wiser to run a lot slower for the first four minutes of the race, and then slowly increase speed to race pace over the next two or three minutes. This opening tactic will reduce muscle glycogen depletion and the lactate build-up that goes with it.

This starting method has only one drawback, and that is when you are running in one of the monster mass marathons when in the first six minutes of the race all sorts of oddities might decide to come past and get in the way, complete with circus props and umbrellas. But it's your day as well as theirs. Just stick to your plan and keep your cool.

The body has an elaborate heat-regulating mechanism which responds quickly to temperature changes, since it tries at all times to maintain a constant temperature. In hot weather there are two adjustments that the body makes, which are very important to runners.

It perspires so that the skin is cooled by evaporation and it also increases the flow of blood to the skin so that the blood can lose heat via the network of small capillaries and veins near the surface.

But blood diverted to the surface is blood diverted away from muscles which need all the fuel they can get. So cooling is all-important.

The key to marathon running is finding the correct pace, and in considering this problem it is helpful to appreciate two somewhat contradictory meanings of 'economy'.

The first meaning is efficiency. The most efficient pace is the pace that uses up the least energy per mile. Unfortunately this is a fast pace, which you may not be able to maintain.

The second meaning is the idea of spending (in this case energy) at a rate you can maintain, a sense of eking out your energy in order to last the distance. Unfortunately, again, this is often a slow or slower pace, and uses up more energy per mile.

While the aim is to finish the race rather than to blow up, if the pace is too slow it brings extra problems in hot and humid weather by way of excessive fluid loss. By not running so quickly you might not heat up so much, but by extending the running time under a hot sun, particularly in humid weather when sweat does not evaporate quickly, you increase the risk of dehydration and heat stroke.

Furthermore, you cannot absorb water as fast as you can lose it when running. Nearly three-quarters of your body is water and in a long run the loss of volume from the blood has to be made up from the rest of the body, and this fluid loss from the cells upsets the body's whole delicate balance.

Yes – finding your right pace is the key to the marathon.

It's All Yours

From now on you're on your own. If it's your first road race or your first time on the fells, or your first fun run or your first Olympic heat, it will be something you're not going to forget. It is your own motivation that has got you to this point – whether over the last weeks or months or years, and it's your own strength of will – as well as the quality of work that you have put into your training – that is going to get you through those next few miles or those next testing laps or the unrelenting four hours of that marathon.

If you have had the stamina to get this far in the book, we are sure you can do the rest. Good luck.

The Running Mind and the Running Body

The scorn felt ten years ago by the early morning businessmen walking through Hyde Park at the sight of the sweat-soaked fitness fanatic (anybody who ran had to be a fanatic) has now changed, if not to the universal pursuit of total fitness, then at least to feelings of guilt among the sedentary, and the certainty that they are taking the trouble, in ever-increasing numbers, to count themselves among the newly converted sweat-soaked hordes.

Now you have joined them. With luck you are well on your way to a new achievement in your running career – a new distance to attempt; a new personal best time to record. Perhaps, if you are a beginner, your first competitive run is looming on the horizon: a somewhat daunting challenge if six months ago you had confined your exercise to chasing buses, but now a challenge you can face with confidence, and with a body which, as we showed in Chapter Three, is already undergoing the changes that go hand in hand with regular exercise.

Already, very soon after you began training, there will have been a strengthening of the muscles exercised, predominantly the legs but also in others in proportion to their use. Some of those significantly involved will have been those used in breathing. It is often overlooked that when running these muscles work much harder, and with a larger range of movement, than they do at rest.

The action of your heart will have improved. The heart is a non-stop muscle which more than any other depends on a plentiful supply of blood, and without developing an even greater supply it cannot in turn pump the extra that an increase in work load demands. Luckily, in order to get more blood to exercised and strengthened muscles, your fine network of capillaries has increased, including those that serve the heart.

Now a strengthened heart can pump an increased amount of blood at each stroke, and so, to do the same amount of work, it does not need to beat so quickly. In turn, a slower-beating heart has more time to fill properly so that it pumps even more per stroke. All physical activity is ultimately limited by the amount of oxygen-rich blood that can be delivered to the muscles, and this increase in the stroke-volume of your heart is basic to fitness.

Besides strengthening the muscles, your running is helping you to get rid of fat in the muscle and fat stored around the body. The reduction in useless body fat together with the greater muscle strength is increasing the power-weight ratio and the body's overall efficiency, and thereby decreasing the load on the heart.

So your lungs are becoming much healthier organs, the airways open up, and breathing is easier because there is less resistance to the passage of air, and the lungs can supply more oxygen to the blood.

The volume of blood also increases in trained runners, and you will gradually be increasing your lung capacity. Result: more oxygen uptake and more blood to circulate it. And a good supply of blood-carrying oxygen and glucose is vital to the brain – another factor in your increased well-being.

This will not all happen at once, and it would do the body no good to try to effect anything but a gradual improvement. Training not only strengthens muscles, but it necessarily strengthens ligaments, tendons and their attachments, and it is obvious that muscles and tendons should develop together: by trying to speed things up, say by using anabolic steroids, it is possible to develop the strength of muscles so quickly that severe damage is done to the tendons and the attachments to the bone which cannot stand the increased loadings. Always develop and train gradually so that the body tunes up uniformly.

Although the response to exercise lessens with age, tests on men aged between fifty-five and seventy have demonstrated significant improvement. These men had been physically inactive for at least twenty years, but after training three to five times per week in one- to two-hour sessions over an eight-week period, their maximum oxygen uptake improved 20 per cent. So it's never too late to start.

With regular exercise, the machine which is your body will be able to work much more efficiently, and thus much longer, without fatigue; and muscles that are regularly and strongly stimulated respond more readily when called upon, and do so with enhanced co-ordination.

Women's muscles and cardiovascular systems and general well-being will be affected in the same way as men's, but there really is a bonus for women who may initially be motivated to run in the hope of improving their figures. They will benefit in three ways: excess fat will be lost by means of diet and exercise; the exercise will consume the fat while preserving the lean tissue; and at the same time muscle tone will improve, posture will improve (especially if the running is accompanied by good flexibility exercises) and previously flabby muscles will improve their shape without any significant increase in size.

Round shoulders, and tummies that look fatter than they are simply because they stick out, will disappear with proper training. Almost invariably, too, an increased circulation enhances the natural complexion and the all-round enhancement of your physical condition puts back the sparkle you thought you had lost.

Not a bad selling point for the men, either.

If the idea of facing an hour's running during a week seems a bit tough on you now, it is because you do not yet know what fitness is like. Running does more than fit you for running – it sets you up for your everyday work, and for your everyday leisure.

And it isn't solely in the more obvious parts of the body that the effects are felt. The brain itself is particularly sensitive to minute chemical changes – very often in a negative sense, producing a wide range of imaginary ailments or psychosomatic illnesses. Drugs or poisons can have strange hallucinatory effects, and when deprived of small amounts of glucose or oxygen the function of the brain is impaired.

The strong healthy heart of a fit person can pump the blood containing enough oxygen and glucose to a brain that will be all the better for it. There are well-documented cases of physical gains being accompanied by emotional improvements and an increased mental alertness.

Vanity is perhaps too strong a word, but whose self-esteem would not be improved if he or she looked better? We all like to be told that we are looking fit and well and if we really know that our muscles are firm, that we have a good posture, that we are not fat and that a good circulation is helping our complexion, then we look out on the world in a much better way.

We have a nervous system of which a part carries out instructions to order, a part which once started continues functioning without being continually instructed, and another part which doesn't wait for conscious instructions at all but issues its own orders. With the central nervous system and the autonomic system so closely interwoven, and given the physiological fact that every cell in the body is connected with the others – the cells of the brain with the cells of the foot – we can be in no doubt that a holistic approach to the mind and the body must be the right one.

Mens Sana . . . ?

This attitude, we feel, is the soundest possible basis for an answer to the often-posed question: Does running have any effect on the mind? It is by no means a simple subject – a series in *Athletics Weekly* magazine by Brian Mitchell on 'Athletes' Minds' in 1982 ran to five parts, which shows there is plenty to say – but the usual dilemma faced in attempting an answer is the old chicken-and-the-egg problem: Was it ultimately the mind that made success possible, or was it the body that allowed the mind to be successful?

It is perhaps the coach, whose job it is to train both mind and body to simultaneous performance and who can watch the results with a certain objectivity, rather than the athlete himself, who can make the most revealing contribution to the debate.

'I have watched four children grow into adults sharing the same environment (house, books music, schools), and I believe strongly that the genetic inheritance is the most important. There is no other way of accounting for the big differences not only between each of them, but also within the pairs (two boys, two girls).

But I do not deny the interaction between the individual and his environment. We all have the power to modify our environment through the free choices that are open to us, and thus modify ourselves at the same time.

Today there are many clichés used on the famous to cut them down to size. They range from "if you can't stand the heat stay out of the kitchen" to "They must like it or they wouldn't do it". They may contain some of the truth, but they certainly do not tell it all.

It does take guts to continue once you have reached the top. Outside observers always seem to be hooked on the motivation problem. After a world record, an Olympic gold, or whatever else strikes them as the pinnacle of success, they all ask, "What is left now to strive for? What can motivate him now?"

There is another big problem. What is hard, and can only get harder all the time, is winning. Not the effort of maintaining the training – that's bad enough – but the knowing that there can never be an unbroken chain of victories. Retiring undefeated looks nice in the record books, but if it is premature retirement purely to get that distinction, then it does not mean quite so much. Every class athlete knows that the last win he has just notched up brings him one race closer to defeat. One man's forty-five consecutive wins only makes the forty-sixth race more desperate.

A world record only makes defeat even more "inexcusable" in the same event at the next championship. There were two winners in the Moscow Games, of whom after all the adulation, it can be said, "only they know the

true cost of their gold". Olympic titles and world records go on exacting a price long after the world thinks they are paid for. There is a common bond between champions and outlaws – both have a big price on their heads.

Carrying that pressure is every bit as tough on the athletes as the training that keeps them there. "I put up with it because I still like winning enough to endure the training. It is nice to have your body working like a 'well-oiled machine', but it is nicer not to go training in mid-winter in the early morning and the late evening with your eyes and ears frozen."

But there is a magic on the big nights which is very hard to describe, for the alchemy of the spectacular in Zurich, say, or Brussels is at the same time both brutal and subtle.

The pre-event interviews with the press and television, the media's incessant hunger for the dramatic announcement like "It's a record attempt tonight", or "I've come here to win the big one" is a maddening part of the scene one could well do without, but without which it wouldn't be the same. The siege of the autograph hunters and the genuine fans, who can make you climb fences to find rear exits from the arena, is only just bearable.

All the year you have been planning for this night. The coach has examined his athlete's progress and condition, changed the emphasis on the training, assessed the performances to date of his athlete and the other contestants and despite all the care in the preparation he accompanies his gladiator (for this is *how* it feels) to the arena knowing that at any time the unthinkable can happen. The long walk from the hotel to the stadium is almost like the walk from death row in an old Warner Brothers movie. Arrival at the warm-up area, often in the semi-darkness away from the track, brings some relief in that the action is beginning at last. The athlete has not eaten for maybe four hours or so, and the coach has starved with him – the one from practicalities, the other from nerves.

No matter how many times you have been there, it only gets harder to bear. The close bond between two people is not without pains, one of which will always be the pain of doubt. The coach is praying that there is nothing that he has not considered and the athlete is carrying the awful load, on top of all the other expectations, of not wanting to fail the coach. The longer you have been successful the greater the pressure you create. No wonder that there comes that moment when even the best have to blurt out: "What the hell am I doing here?"

Then it's through the tunnel and into the arena. The floodlights are on and, surrounded by flash guns and tracked by television cameras, the gladiator is presented to the crowd.

For him it is the Greyhound Derby, the Heavyweight Championship, the World Cup Final and Barnum & Bailey's all in one. Suddenly he is going to lay on the line thousands of hours of training and thousands of miles of running for a spin of the wheel that may only last one minute and forty odd seconds.

What is the immediate reward? The chance to lose and slip away into oblivion (but not if the world says he should have won). Or win and hope that he can get up enough strength to face the ensuing fracas which can only be likened to a coroner's court being held during a wild coronation.

When the magic moment does come, that instant when the "well-oiled machine" goes into overdrive and the field fades, there is only the exultation of the final drive for the line . . . unless the trackside clock is in view, when the seconds go too quickly and the tape starts to recede, prolonging the agony of the record attempt even further.

Why then do they go on? The answer surely can only be that the desire to be the best, the *numero uno*, that made them what they are in the first place, is still there.

Pride also plays a part. "I will not hang around after my best is no longer good enough – I will walk off the track and stay off." Who can argue with Seb on that?

And if anyone should ask us "Is it worth all that?" the answer is still yes.

It all comes back, it seems, to motivation. In a television interview with Seb, David Coleman once said that some runners were motivated by the opposition, "but you seem to be self-motivated. How do you do it?" Seb's reply was: "I suppose it's the motivation of just wanting to go out and run faster than I have run before, and hopefully faster than anyone else has run, and that gives me a lot of pleasure. It's sitting down before a race and feeling that at the end of the evening I may have achieved something really special."

The motivation of wanting to run faster or further than you have run before can apply to anyone. Victory is very worthwhile when it is victory over yourself, and at the end of the day the knowledge that you have had the will to force yourself to climb another few places up the finishing list can be something special to you.

So whether or not you dream of life at the top, cherish that certificate, keep that bronze medal, they are part of you. They say that you too have tried.

There were two races as a boy up Frodsham Hill and back that were Olympian in endeavour. In an old photograph of the first race there is to be seen all the agony of a Calvary.

To compete means that you are submitting yourself to a test. In fact you are being examined. In a Britain which for too long has lost its way in a distortion of egalitarianism, testing, particularly of the young, has become a dirty word. We need to unlearn this attitude.

To hang on to the end, to force your way to the front and win a desperately hard fought race needs tremendous determination, and to run flat out to the end knowing that victory has gone is hardly any easier.

To compete takes courage, and courage, as distinct from foolhardiness, is an act of will.'

Ultimately, successful running is a conquest of the body by the mind.

By successful running we mean the winning of major titles by the stars *and* winning the battle to maintain the meaningful fitness schedules that the forty-plus runners have set themselves. The battle may have to be fought much harder by some than by others but then life is not always fair, and having the will to see it through and practising that will is a quality everyone can aspire to.

Every time a runner goes out for his run, that is an act of will, and every time he finishes the run he will feel himself a better man for it. The worse the weather, the greater the willpower required, and the more the will is exercised the stronger it becomes. Smugness is not a pleasant characteristic, but anyone who submits himself to a hard discipline and sticks it out has a right to be pleased with himself. The experience belongs to him – it is his bit of individuality and his bit of success – success achieved with will, with thought and with concentration.

If all this seems a bit heavy, then consider the lighter side. Pleasures simple or intellectual are not enjoyed very much when accompanied by dyspepsia, constipation and lassitude. Dragging around a poor body takes the joy out of everything from bingo to chess. Poor old Karl Marx is alleged to have said that his writing would give the bourgeoisie cause to remember his boils.

Take your pick of the old sayings – 'Blowing the cobwebs out of your mind', 'Getting some fresh air in your lungs' and the like.

From the Ancient Greeks until today, bodily health has been considered indispensable to mental health. It has been said that nothing succeeds like success, and certainly earning your own self-respect is your own success story.

At school Seb was a very modest scholar, but as soon as he found himself as a runner and started winning races his school work started improving. Even the great chess champions now know that they have to prepare for the big intellectual battle of the world title with a carefully thought-out regime of physical fitness.

So if willpower is mind-power and running can exercise the will, then surely running can improve the mind.

'Running is much more than a convenient way of "improving the mind" and keeping the body healthy.

For me it has been my life, and I hope it will go on being my life. Running now is work and excitement and tension and a challenge, as it has been ever since I started competing seriously at the age of fourteen. But when I have retired from competition, running will be contentment and relaxation and pleasure.

When I do retire, I think the break is going to have to be a clean one. For any athlete who has competed at world class it's very difficult to take a voluntary step down and compete at less than best. I really can't see myself two years after retirement running in my club's Christmas Handicap, or making up the numbers in a local cross-country race, or running my leg in the inter-club road relays. If the break is going to be healthy, it's got to be a break right across the board.

But running will certainly be there, and there is a lot of running that I want to do that I couldn't possibly do now. I watched the London Marathon earlier this year, when I was cheering on a friend, and the atmosphere really did affect me, it was very moving – not just the fast men at the front, but all the men and women down the field. They seemed to get such support from each other, in the easy miles early on, and in the shared pain and struggle towards the end. I'm sure I'll run a marathon one day – not to win, just to take part with everyone else.

I'll be free of programmes and schedules and stop-watches, too, when I've retired. If it's cold and raining when I get up in the morning, I can put off my run till the next day. And, in a funny way, I'll be able to take more risks. I can run across terrain that it would be mad for me to run across now – moorland paths, places like that, where the risk to legs and ankles and muscles have been too great.

I won't be inhibited in that way any more. I can just keep in shape and run and enjoy every minute of it.'

Appendix

Joining a Club

Not everyone will want to join a club, but they have their advantages – not only for the companionship, the coaching and the competition, but also for the fact that membership of a club is likely to allow you reduced entry fees to many events, and even get you a discount at your local sportswear shop. A letter to any of the following, accompanied by a stamped addressed envelope, will get you a list of the clubs in your area, and the address and telephone number of the secretary.

Athletics Clubs
All clubs affiliated to the Amateur Athletic Association are grouped in regions:
Southern Counties AAA and *England and Wales Women's AAA* Francis House, Francis Street, London SW1 1DL.
Midland AAA Devonshire House, High Street, Deritend, Birmingham B12 0LP.
Northern Counties AAA Studio 44, Bluecoat Chambers, Liverpool L1 BXC3.
Welsh AAA 54 Charles Street, Cardiff.
Scottish AAA and Scottish Women's AAA 16 Royal Crescent, Glasgow G3 7SL.
Northern Ireland AAA 20 Kernan Park, Portadown, Co. Armagh, N. Ireland.
Northern Ireland Women's AAA Tir na Nog, Old Calgorm Road, Ballymena, N. Ireland.
Irish Republic (Bord Luthleas na Eireann) BLE Offices, 69 Jones Road, Dublin 3.

Veterans' Athletics
Men become veterans at 40, women at 35, and there are many athletic clubs and athletic events run specially for them, as well as classes reserved for them in many open races. Members generally join the Veterans' Association for their area if they want to compete.

Parent body: *British Veterans Athletic Federation* Hon Sec Jack Haslam, 10 Higher Dunscar, Egerton, Bolton, Lancs.

Cross-Country
The area Cross-Country Association will provide a list of local clubs.

Eastern Counties Cross-Country Association. Hon Sec C. C. Bruning, 15 Karen Close, Ipswich, Suffolk IP1 4LP.
Midland Counties Cross-Country Association Hon Sec B. B. Heatley, 6 Kirkstone Crescent, Wombourne, near Wolverhampton.
Northern Cross-Country Association Hon Sec J. E. Davies, 14 Neal Avenue, Heald Green, Cheadle, Cheshire.
East Lancashire Cross-Country Association Hon Sec C. E. Haslam, 10 Higher Dunscar, Egerton, Bolton, Lancs.
West Lancashire Cross-Country Association Hon Sec Dr P. R. Thomas, 5 Newby Avenue, Rainhill, Prescot, Merseyside.
Yorkshire Cross-Country Association Hon Sec J. E. Smith, 7 Birch Avenue, Bradford, West Yorkshire BD5 8EZ.

North-Eastern Counties Cross Country Association Hon Sec M. Frazer, 11 Heslop Drive, Darlington, Co. Durham.

Southern Counties Cross-Country Association Hon Sec H. J. Hicks, 34 The Crescent, Friern Barnet, London N11 3HH.

Scottish Cross-Country Union Hon Sec J. E. Clifton, 38 Silvermowers Drive, Edinburgh EH4 5MM.

Welsh Cross-Country Association Mrs I. Lisle, 38 Nantfawr Road, Cyncoed, Cardiff.

Northern Ireland Cross-Country Association (as Northern Ireland AAA).

Orienteering

A full calendar of events, for anyone wishing to give orienteering a try, is available from:

British Orienteering Federation National Office, 41 Dale Road, Matlock, Derbyshire DE4 3LT.

You are able to try a couple of events as an 'independent', but should you wish to orienteer regularly you could be required to join a club, which would be affiliated at the same time to the area orienteering association and the national federation.

Fell Running

Members of the *Fell Runners Association* receive a full fixture list.

Membership secretary: N. F. Berry, 165 Penistone Road, Kirkburton, Huddersfield HD8 0PH.

Reading and Reference

While some of the following publications are inevitably more detailed and specialised than others, we have found them all valuable in their way over the years.

Training Theory by Frank Dick (British Amateur Athletics Board)
The Physiology of Exercise by Morehouse and Miller (C. V. Mosby)
Run, Run, Run by Fred Wilt (Track and Field News)
A Scientific Approach to Distance Running by David L. Costill (Track and Field News)
The Aerobics Way by Kenneth H. Cooper (Corgi)
The Complete Middle Distance Runner by Watts, Wilson and Horwill (Stanley Paul)
The Challenge of the Marathon by Cliff Temple (Stanley Paul)
Orienteering by Brian Porteus (Oxford University Press)
Tackle Orienteering by John Disley (Stanley Paul)
The Penguin Book of Orienteering by Roger Smith (Penguin)

Fitness, Health and Work Capacity ed. Leonard A. Larson (Macmillan)
Textbook of Work Physiology by Astrand and Rodahl (McGraw-Hill)
Strength Training for Athletes by R. J. Pickering (B.A.A.B.)

Mobility Exercises by Peter Harper (B.A.A.B.)
Fit to Exercise by Burke and Humphreys (Pelham)
Human Movement by Joseph R. Higgins (C. V. Mosby)
The Running Body (Runners World, booklet 27)

Success in Nutrition by Magnus Pyke (John Murray)
Diet in Sport by Wilf Paish (E.P. Publishing)
Teaching Nutrition and Food Sciences by Margaret Knight (Batsford)

The Athlete's Guide to Sports Medicine by Ellington Darden (Contemporary Books Inc.)
The Penguin Medical Encyclopaedia (Penguin)
Encyclopaedia of Athletics Medicine (Runners World, booklet 12)
The Sports Health Handbook by Harris, Lovesey and Oram (World's Work)
The Sunday Times New Book of Body Maintenance (Mermaid Books)

Photographic Acknowledgements

Allsport: 1, 5, 41, 51, 63, 80, 181; *Associated Newspapers*: 123; *Olympus Sports*: 145, 148–49; *Mark Shearman*: 2 (right), 9, 18, 25, 35–9, 53, 66–71, 83, 101, 143, 154, 155; *Sheffield Newspapers*: 26; *Sunday Times*: (Chris Smith) 7; *UPI*: vi–vii, 161, 182–83.

Index